An Inexact Science of the Heart

An Inexact Science of the Heart

Essays

Alfred DePew

Dog Star Press
Vancouver, BC
CANADA

for my father

Sometimes a man stands up during supper
and walks outdoors, and keeps on walking,
because of a church that stands somewhere in the East.
And his children say blessings on him as if he were dead.
And another man, who remains inside his own house,
stays there, inside the dishes and in the glasses,
so that his children have to go far out into the world
toward that same church which he forgot.

— Rainer Maria Rilke
(Robert Bly, trans.)

and for Sequoia

who knew my heart as well
as anyone in this world

An Inexact Science of the Heart

Introduction by Agnes Bushell

Published by Dog Star Press
Vancouver, BC

Which is to say, if you're quoting me, please cite the source
– just like you learned in high school – remember?
Don't steal my work. I won't steal yours.
It's a deal, OK?

"Sometimes a man stands up during supper"
Selected Poems of Rainer Maria Rilke:
A Translation from the German and Commentary by Robert Bly
(New York: Harper & Row, Publishers, 1981)

Excerpts from Rainer Maria Rilke's letters
are from *Letters on Cézanne* edited by Clara Rilke
(New York: Fromm International Publishing Corporation, 1985).
Translated by Joel Agee.

Walt Whitman, excerpt from "The Dear Love of Comrades"
(New York: W.W. Norton & Company, Inc., 1968).

The short pieces and parts of some of the longer essays
first appeared in different forms in my column
"Just Between Us" in the Vancouver Observer.

ISBN 978-1-0689826-0-6
eBook 978-1-0689826-1-3

Cover image: "Liquid Heart" Bavand Keshavarz
Wiki Science Competition 2021
https://commons.wikimedia.org/wiki/File:Liquid_Heart.jpg

Contents

Also by Alfred DePew

The Melancholy of Departure

Wild and Woolly: A Journal Keeper's Handbook

A Wedding Song for Poorer People

Odalisque

Migrant cultural worker, writer, painter, and process facilitator, Alfred DePew has taught at the Universities of Vermont and New Hampshire, the Maine College of Art, and Haystack Mountain School of Crafts. His writing workshops have been sponsored by The Maine Writers and Publishers Alliance and various community programs throughout the United States and Canada. He served for a number of years on the faculty of the Center for Right Relationship (CRR Global) as individual supervisor, certification cohort leader, front of room leader, and director of supervision. He lives in Vancouver, BC where he offers spiritual accompaniment, astrological consultations, energy work, and on-going support for community leaders, clergy, writers, artists, intutitives, and healing arts practitioners.

Liberal Arts Faculty, Maine College of Art, circa 2000

Front row left to right: Candice Kanes, Agnes Bushell,
Camille Trabanco, Alfred DePew
Back row left to right: Dana Sawyer, Bob Jenkins, Claude Caswell

Introduction

I don't remember the first time I met Alfred DePew, though I suspect it was at a meeting of the Liberal Arts Department of the Portland School of Art (now Maine College of Art), and if that were the case, it would have occurred at the home of the department chair, a poet who lived in a wealthy suburb of the city. I don't think Alfred had a car in those days, so I may have driven him there and back, and I imagine we would have laughed a good deal coming and going because that's something we always do together: laugh. In any case, our meeting would have taken place around 1985. And now that I write that date, I have to rub my eyes and look at it again. Is it possible that Alfred and I have been friends for nearly forty years? I suppose it is.

Friendship – the making of friends, the keeping of them, the richness they add to one's life, the grief accompanying their loss – is one of the subjects of *An Inexact Science of the Heart,* this amazing collection of essays you hold in your hands. Friendship is an art, and the talent for friendship may well be like the talent for drawing. Alfred, in one essay, describes it as "a proclivity, a desire, a hunger for something, ... a willingness and a curiosity."

That Alfred exceeds in this art of friendship can be seen from the first essay in the book, "Finding Poems." The story is simple. He finds a letter, abandoned on a bench, a "return to sender" label over the address. The envelope has been ripped open, and Alfred sees that the contents are poems, written in a language he cannot read. He takes the poems home, prepares a new envelope, and sends the poems back to the writer, someone he will never know and who will never know him.

From that first essay, Alfred's curious and sympathetic eye turns to his own family. They were, he writes, "a rogue's gallery of dreamers, drinkers, jailbirds, patriots, heretics, non-conformists, arch-conservatives and social reformers." He introduces us to his parents, delightful characters for the reader if not for their children, and to his siblings and cousins. "My mother always said the DePews were the nuttiest bunch of people she had ever met." Nutty they might be, but I loved meeting them here on these pages: his mother, a forgetful woman who couldn't remember how she had met her husband; his father, whose bedtime stories were flying lessons, imaginative trips to places like Chicago's Museum of Science and Industry; and his cousin Thomas, the family historian, "a clean-cut suburban James Dean" whose life changed when he realized by "the hard judgement of the soul by the soul" that he had not done what he had been put on earth to do.

In the course of this book, we meet many of Alfred's friends, his lovers and guides, his teachers. They are an astonishing variety of people, each drawn with such art that they seem capable of stepping off the page for a deep conversation with you in your own living room. We meet actors and artists, lesbian activists and activist nuns, drinkers and writers and rabbis and mystics and astrologers. We travel with Alfred to St. Louis in November 2014, and are there the day the grand jury refuses to indict the white police officer who shot and killed Michael Brown. We are with him in Louisville for the Spiritual Directors International Conference. We listen in on his conversations with his students and with his mentors. We glimpse, in passing, the writers Carolyn Chute, Dianne Benedict, and Donald Murray.

And all the time we are traveling with Alfred on his quest to find his soul's true home, we watch him trying various beliefs on for size, finding they all fit him. He says, "I follow a path that makes itself known to me only if I keep on walking." A Protestant by birth, he explores Sufism, Judaism, and many New Age philosophies and practices before settling on Catholicism. Yet even as he practices the Ignatian Spiritual Exercises, he accepts belief in reincarnation, not exactly a Catholic article of faith. He believes because he has had an actual experience – in a park in Leningrad. I will not spoil this for you, but it is one of my favorite moments in the book.

"This is a story about family stories," Alfred writes early on, and he means it is also a story about the far-reaching effect of those stories on his own life, and how many years it took him to understand them and make peace with them. It is a story about America's stories as well, for, with the exception of Native people, we are a country of immigrants, of people who fled, and brought their stories, good and bad, along with them. It is the story of a man's life, and so also the story of the past seventy years of American history, the story of how this particular man, Alfred DePew, navigated, maneuvered, survived, and even thrived, and how he experienced the major events of that time. From the perspective of American history, the fact that Alfred has lived the last sixteen years as a citizen of a different country – that he chose, like his own ancestors, to be an immigrant – is telling indeed.

Alfred mentions his house in Portland only once in this book. The home he searches for is not a building, and certainly not a small house in Portland, Maine. But I remember when he bought his house on Pine Street, and I remember going to Liberal Arts Department meetings there, because he offered it and because, being in town, it was much easier to get to than driving into the rich suburbs. He had a sign up on his door asking guests to take their shoes off before they came in, an unusual request at the time. Whenever I pass that house now, I think of Alfred, a continent away in another country. I miss him, and so I treasure *An Inexact Science of the Heart* as a gift from him. When I read it, I hear his voice. As adept as he is in the art of friendship, he has made it easy for every reader who picks up this book to get to know him. You can dip in anywhere and meet him – in St Louis, or in Palm Springs, in London or Leningrad or Vancouver – or you can read from beginning to end, watching the story unfold, one episode after another. Either way, you will find yourself in good hands. "A story worth its salt always has more than one version," he will tell you, and, of course, you will believe him. It is hard-won knowledge, and it is coming from a friend.

Agnes Bushell
Portland, Maine
July 2024

Finding Poems

When I sit down on the bench outside, I see a sheet of notebook paper with writing on it. The sheet has been unfolded, and the writing might be Polish. A poem, by the look of it. I lean over to see if I can spot whoever might have left it, but there's no one around.

Someone so moved or offended—devastated by impossibility, or annoyed by the attention—simply walked off without it. Or so I imagine.

I hesitate to pick up something so intimate, and yet I feel I have to. There are five poems on three sheets of paper. Then I see the envelope they've been torn out of. A Canada Post "Return to Sender" label covers the address.

I imagine the poet, confident that the poems are on their way, their intended recipient waiting. Or will they be a surprise? And a welcomed one or unwelcomed?

I assume they are love poems, but they may not be.

In my hand, I hold five distinct moments, each with its own title, saying something intended for someone else. Private. Suddenly I feel worse than the thief who stole them, and tearing open the envelope, discarded them because there was no money.

I can't bring myself to drop them into the nearby trash bin, so I decide to become a messenger, the poet's friend and ally. I think of all those who have carried poems from emperor to courtesan, from confidant to queen. A job not without its dangers. Pages tucked into a doublet or sewn into the lining of a vest to get them across hostile borders.

Secret. Hidden.

How many poems have traveled this way and never arrived? Something tender and vulnerable is imperiled here—the contents of a poet's heart, too often lost.

The writing on the envelope is hard to read. A nervous hurried, scrawl. There's not even a stamp.

W. H. Auden once said, "poetry makes nothing happen," but how can that be so? Seduction. Marriage. Infidelity. Revolution. Poems carry subtle and urgent messages from one private chamber to another. I think of the world described in The Tale of Genji in eleventh-century Japan. Or eight lines scribbled by Simone de Beauvoir on a napkin to Jean-Paul Sartre at Les Deux Magots nine hundred years later. Or Anna Akhmatova addressing Marina Tsvetaeva in verse under the Soviets.

Poems of love, admiration, admonition, scorn, longing. A secret code, a puzzle, a riddle designed to befuddle the gestapo, or the czar's police, or the KGB. Safe, each poem a world unto itself, open only to initiates.

The poems in my hand are in a language I cannot read, but I know enough to know they are important—to the poet if to no one else.

And so I carry them upstairs and address a new envelope in my own square hand: To the Poet who resides at . . . and then the address as best I can make it out, trusting in Destiny, the Muses, and all Protective Spirits of the Art of Poetry that the poems will return to the poet and that the poet will perform the next necessary act of faith.

The Gospel of Thomas

the strange idea of family
travelling through the flesh

– Carlos Drummond de Andrade
"Family Portrait"
(Elizabeth Bishop, trans.)

My mother always said the DePews were the nuttiest bunch of people she'd ever met. She had a point. I come from a long line of very strange people. Especially the men. A veritable rogues' gallery of dreamers, drinkers, jailbirds, patriots, heretics, nonconformists, archconservatives, and social reformers. Conspicuously absent are Sephardic Jews, Trotskyists, Catholics, and queers.

So God created me.

The ancient ones remind us that if our story ceases to be alive, ceases to instruct and heal us with its wisdom, we forget who we are and our culture dies. I think of Scheherazade and the stories she tells the king to save her own life and the lives of other women, stories that in the course of a thousand and one nights soften a tyrant's heart and transform him into a wise ruler and loving husband. Stories like these remind us that we are not in charge, that what we see in waking life and touch with our hands is not all there is. Something else makes itself known to us out of the corner or our eye, in the deep forest, or in our night visions that come from we know not where and recall stories about Sky Woman, Inanna, Orpheus, and Persephone.

This is a story about family stories, not the stories themselves so much as how they change in the telling, expand and shrink, or get buried and then resurface in a tall clay jar in the Egyptian desert. Gnostic gospels, skeletons in the family closet, dry bones just waiting for sinews, flesh, and breath. This is a story about how we fall out of our own story and get drawn back into its mythic dimensions, full of the mystery we keep trying to explain away, but which is invoked anew whenever someone says "Once upon a time," and we step through the looking glass or out of the back of an old wardrobe, where it happens to be snowing when, in the world on the other side, it was summer, and we encounter a faun who goes by the name of Mr. Tumnus.

My cousin Thomas was a bit like that magical figure in C. S. Lewis's Narnia. When I was growing up, Thomas seemed to be in a world apart, and not just because he was seven years older or because of his striking appearance—he had his mother's blond hair and something of her radiance, for there was really no other word for the light she generated when she entered a room. It was something else, all his own, a wildness of spirit, the alertness of a young deer ready at any moment to leap back into the trees of another realm. A trickster like Puck or Pan, with the quicksilver mind of Hermes. Naturally rebellious, there was nonetheless something urgent, principled, and noble about his idealism—and something faintly tragic. For eccentricity had become increasingly dangerous in the America of the 1950s, and Thomas was particularly vulnerable to wounding.

I remember him standing in the middle of a room full of people, a tweed jacket draped over the wide shoulders of his slender frame. He was back in St. Louis for Thanksgiving break in his second year of college in Connecticut with long hair and a full red beard. To me he was the epitome of an East Coast sophistication I feared I would never manage, as later in my room I tried walking with a sport coat on my shoulders, but it slid right off. Aloof and detached, Thomas was making pronouncements about art, culture, and politics. I stood at a distance, watching to see how this would go over with the family. It was common knowledge that his father was furious about the beard, but it was Thomas's attitude that seemed to vex my uncle even more—a sign of insubordination, disloyalty if not to God, then to the nation, which in 1965, with the escalation of the Vietnam War, was the greater heresy. My uncle's men friends and business associates called my cousin a peacenik. The women called him arty and affected, favorite put-downs of the era, loaded with sexual innuendo. At thirteen, I had learned to read signs and portents and to chart the emotional undercurrents in a room of grown-ups. Subtly, silently, my cousin Thomas was under attack, and I paid close attention from just outside the line of fire. He was finding his way out of a world that I was only just beginning to understand was closing in around me.

By 1975, Thomas had filed for conscientious objector status, failed to appear for a meeting at his draft board, been wanted by the FBI, somehow managed to sort all of that out and fulfill his alternative service. He had rented a loft first in New York and then in New Jersey and produced an extensive body of large poured paintings on raw canvas inspired by a series of visionary experiences. He had become interested in underground films and had started to photograph people in the streets between three and five in the morning, when, as he said, "it was safe for the freaks to come out." On a trip to the Middle East to photograph Berber herdsmen, he was abducted in Beirut and kept for a week in a basement, where, convinced that he was going to be gassed to death, he came to realize that he had to make peace with his father, and was suddenly released into bright sunlight the next morning through the efforts of a mercenary soldier he had met along the way and a mysterious princess who paid his ransom.

Meanwhile, I managed to make it through high school, which was touch and go there for a while, registered for the Selective Service as a conscientious objector on my eighteenth birthday, made it into a progressive liberal arts college in Wisconsin, and drew a high number in the first draft lottery, which meant I was relieved of any responsibility to do alternative service. I traveled in Europe, worked in a bookstore in England for nine months, and returned to St. Louis to finish my undergraduate degree at an even more progressive college. I won a teaching assistantship in the north of France and was preparing my final escape from St. Louis as Thomas returned to live permanently, as it turned out, and to become the guardian and narrator of the family history once his father died in 1992.

I visited my uncle to make my own peace with him in 1990. I had settled in Maine, gotten sober and wanted to make amends for anything I had done to hurt him when I was drinking. I had cut myself off from family members and failed to acknowledge my uncle's many gestures of loving generosity and support in the years my father struggled with his own drinking. Alcoholism had been part of our story for generations, the bête noire lurking in the shadows. As we talked, I sensed a weight lift from my uncle's shoulders when he told me how he had tried for years to get my father sober without success. Together we were breaking an ancient curse, and I could feel one sorrow after another being released from the hearts of our ancestors stretching back centuries.

Thomas and I didn't reconnect until a few years later when I began what became for me a yearly migration between Maine, where I taught in the fall and winter, and northern New Mexico, where I wrote and taught in the summer. I would drive through St. Louis on my way out and back, and I always made time to meet Thomas at the coffee shop near his apartment. I often found him writing on a pad of yellow paper or in a small notebook, at work on the family chronicles. His beard was wild and bushy and mostly gray. He wore his signature threadbare tweed jacket, its sleeves patched at the elbow. On his head a soft-brimmed gray hat. He spoke in the slow, even rhythms of a metronome, each word, each detail given equal weight, his gaze fixed somewhere above my head and to my left. Determined and deliberate as they were, the stories were also fluid, following an elliptical orbit from Lebanon to Languedoc, to New York City and Brazil. They took on the enigmatic character of parable and the teaching stories of Hassidic rabbis and Sufi masters. Stories of rascally mischief, loyalty, honor, tyranny, outwitted for a time if not defeated, fortunes made then lost—all somehow leading to solid middle-class respectability, a message Thomas delivered with a wry smile that always put me in mind of Anton Chekhov.

Thomas had something of a following at the coffee shop, younger people, some of them artists; others were hipsters with New Age sensibilities. They knew his schedule, and they came to listen. They loved him, accepted him as he was, and appreciated his wisdom. They questioned and challenged him, laughed with him—engaged in genuine dialogue. Not one of them treated him as an oddball or a freak, as I confess I sometimes had over the years.

By now, Thomas had woven parts of his own story into the family legend, including his captivity in the Beirut dungeon. In all our striving for self-improvement and transcendence, my family seemed to lose sight of the downward movement of the soul—into the body, into earth's underbrush, across the River Styx, and into the domain of Pluto. Convinced that he was going to die, Thomas received what he called "a hard judgment of the soul by the soul" that he had failed to do what he had been put on earth to do. Though less literal, my descent into the netherworld of grief after my father's death was every bit as life-changing as Thomas's sudden release from captivity in that the world we both reentered was transfigured in ways that defy description in conventional language. "Conversion of the Mind / Like Sanctifying in the Soul— / Is witnessed—not explained—" says Emily Dickinson.

As much as Thomas loved philosophical discourse, he was first and foremost a painter, and painting was in a real sense his first language. He identified the purpose of what he called his "resurrected life" as "the reconciliation of opposites toward the resolution of conflict" which resulted in various projects promoting nonviolence and sustainability. To my mind, the paintings he produced before 1975 spoke to the metaphysics of those later projects and suggest that the visionary experiences which inspired them revealed a unified and coherent consciousness that stretches far beyond most of Western philosophy and suggests a knowing, or gnosis, that we find in the work of mystics and poets.

Thomas's paintings made me think of outer space. There is an emanation of light in the one I have that seems to open into deep infinity—somehow moving forward and receding at the same time. Something in the darker shape to the left of that light suggests embodiment, a portal, the delta of Venus, forming itself out of the body of a cloud. The moment when spirit interpenetrates matter or dematerializes and returns to essence.

Though Thomas never associated himself with color-field painters like Morris Lewis and Helen Frankenthaler, his method was related to theirs. He poured paint onto raw canvas and let it go where it flowed. He made acrylics act like watercolor, remarkably subtle and nuanced with nothing of the harsh sheen that acrylic paint often has. Many of the paintings were large, and it was as if one stood inside clouds—churning, unfolding, expanding, and contracting all at once—in the powerful presence of an oncoming storm, and at the same time filled with peace and a sense of wonder. An art critic once visited his loft, looked around at the empty walls, and asked where the paintings were. "You're standing on them," said Thomas, who had spread them all out carefully on the floor.

Apparently, Thomas was not the first painter in the family. Our grandmother took classes from the painter and poet Frederick Oakes Sylvester who taught at her high school and later at Principia College. And a painting by Thomas's father hung in the front hall of his apartment. I don't know how old Uncle Tom was when he painted the landscape. What impressed me was not only its accuracy and the precise handling of the paint, it was the energy and spirit it conveyed.

As strange as Thomas was, he had always managed to fit in better than I had. He was a good student, a good athlete, well liked, and, as I mentioned earlier, a bit of a rebel. He was also moody and sullen at times, a kind of clean-cut suburban James Dean without the cigarette pack rolled into his T-shirt sleeve. He had always been part of the family story, and I had always felt myself to be outside of it somehow, as though I'd been blackballed in a Masonic vote at birth. I often wondered what I was doing in that family. So did a Jewish friend's mother who exclaimed one afternoon, "Those people are not your people," recalling the story of Ruth and Naomi, and I did feel a strange familiarity when I sat down to my first Seder with that family and heard the youngest daughter answer the four questions in Hebrew. Years later, I was studying the Torah with a rabbi in Maine. He was sure I was descended from Sephardic Jews who had migrated to France to escape the Inquisition. "But rabbi," I said, "it doesn't make sense. Why would we join the French Protestants when they were in as much danger from the Catholics as the Jews were?"

"Just because you're Jewish," he said, "doesn't mean you're smart."

Before we became Huguenots, we may have been involved with

a twelfth-century Gnostic sect. According to Thomas, one of our ancestors, "the ruler of Languedoc," defended "the right of the Cathars to believe what they chose," and in doing so "gave up his position and his fortune." When I read about the Cathars, I was struck by their contempt for the material world, the earth itself, and the body. They were said to believe in two deities—a good God, the creator of spirit; and an evil God, the God of the Israelites, who created the physical world. Their idea was to renounce the material self and world in order to return to their angelic origins through a rite that made them a Perfect. While Thomas never said that our ancestor agreed with the Cathars, I recognized some disturbing family patterns—a chronic and crippling perfectionism and superiority, an undercurrent of shame, a devaluing of the physical in favor of the intellectual and spiritual, never mind anti-Semitism. To be sure, these patterns belong to Christian colonialist culture in general, but they found particular expressions in my family and in me.

I listened to Thomas's stories for clues about what had formed my own thinking and cultural identity, as well as for the origins of my alcoholism. I heard something else in them as well—an unmistakable trace of the untamed, instinctual, something wild, alive, full of joy, but also a howling sorrow. Where had it gone, this wildness? How had it become so muffled, its spirit broken and harnessed to plow and carriage?

Some said that Thomas seemed more remote, less alive after 1975. He had lost his youthful radiance. But I think it receded somewhere deep within, where it could shine safely, away from people's scorn, a place where he was most alive, set apart from an increasingly violent and vulgar world. His equanimity was close to perfect, but one sensed the work it took to maintain it. As he grew older, he ate less, grew thinner, lighter, and more porous it seemed with every year, as though he were in the process of disappearing into one of his own paintings.

And something in me was becoming more vivid and alive. Sobriety had landed me in my body, a shock in and of itself, and it insisted I not override its pain, its pleasure, or its wisdom—a gradual and often daunting process, which prompted me to study dance and massage, as I continued to teach, write, travel, and publish. The more access I had to myself, the larger my world became, and none of this would have happened had I not grieved my father's death and encountered my own soul in the process. Gradually, I began to see that I belonged to a family of people who had never really fit in, no matter how good they were at appearing to do so.

As it turns out, Thomas's father inducted me into the family by accident. He was in the hospital. No one was supposed to know he was dying, but my brother-in-law let it slip in a phone call, so the next day I booked a seat on an early flight to St. Louis, rented a car, drove directly to the hospital, and walked into my uncle's room unannounced—and uninvited—with the headstrong determination of so many of my ancestors. He turned and said, "What are you doing here? You're not supposed to arrive for another three chapters." I laughed and said, "Well, I'm early." We had the kind of conversation one has with someone on morphine, and I took his hand as he described, without any consternation or fear, the crows gathering in a corner of the room. After a while, I stood up, kissed his forehead, and drove back to the airport. He died a week or so later, on my fortieth birthday and the publication date of my first collection of stories—written on the typewriter he had given me for my high-school graduation.

A story worth its salt, a story with its full mythological potency, always has more than one version—it has to in order to come alive and speak to the time in which it is being retold. All true storytellers know this. It's the lawyers and clerics who get tangled up in which is the right version. There is of course the question of fact. When another cousin, a certified genealogist, let it be known that she could find no actual evidence connecting us to Languedoc, or even to Chauncey Depew, a noted after-dinner speaker and US Senator from New York, I shook my head and said, "Jody, you'll never discover the truth about a DePew if you rely on facts alone. The real story lies in another dimension. You'd have better luck finding scientific proof of the birth of Aphrodite or Athena."

I was in St. Louis for a book event in November 2014, and I met Thomas for coffee in the usual place. I was staying with another cousin who urged me to invite Thomas to their house for Thanksgiving dinner. For some reason these cousins didn't talk—Thomas was hard to reach by phone and he almost never answered emails—but I suspected one of those family estrangements whose origin nobody remembers. I arranged to pick him up on the day and drive him to the gathering. It is the custom to have the eldest read a poem about gratitude our grandfather had written to bless the meal. That year, it was Thomas, and he fairly beamed as he recited it from memory. I thought of all the people who had died and yet seemed to be present as I looked around the table and wondered what my cousin Steve's children and grandchildren thought of these two weird bachelors, distant cousins from another time. I remembered being their age and pondering our great-aunts, two ancient maiden ladies in baggy dresses and sensible shoes who appeared at holidays, the outermost planets in the family solar system, barely visible but nonetheless exerting a mysterious influence. When the visit was over, I drove Thomas home, waited until he had opened the door to his building, and returned his wave.

The day after the news reached me of his death five years later, I was working at my desk and stood up to stretch. I felt an effervescence spiral up through the right side of my body. "Thomas," I cried. "You old fox. It's you, isn't it." The feeling of his presence lasted about twenty minutes, and in the days and weeks that followed, I considered the mystery of my cousin and the stories he told, and how he and I became woven into them however tangentially. I thought of his presence at Thanksgiving, reciting our grandfather's poem, whatever it was that had kept these two cousins from speaking, set aside if not forgotten. And I thought of my friend's family in high school, the place they set for me at Seder, and could almost feel Thomas's hands on my head in blessing, whispering the question that begins the Passover meal: "Why is this night different from all other nights?"

And so, once again, we tell the story of bitter herbs, of Exodus, and of everything that followed.

Saturn and the Flying Boy

My father taught me how to leave my body. He could leave his even when he wasn't drunk. I'd watch him do it at the dinner table. Swift, subtle, like Houdini slipping out of a pair of handcuffs, he'd simply step away. I learned to fine-tune my senses, to track my father's heartbeat with my pulse, and to taste in my own mouth that sweet freedom that was on my father's tongue. And then I knew. He was gone, hovering somewhere nearby, even as his head nodded and his face smiled, pretending to listen. Psychologists call this disassociation, a response to trauma. My dad and I didn't need anything life-threatening to trigger our departure. It could be simple stupidity, unpleasantness, or just plain boredom—anything unworthy of our attention, and we'd be off.

His bedtime stories were flying lessons. He'd tuck me in and ask where I wanted to go.

"Anywhere?"

"Anywhere at all."

"Even Chicago?"

"Especially Chicago!" he'd cry. And with a head nod and a whistle, he'd summon Johnny West Wind in through the window, whether it was open or not. We hopped on his back and Johnny West Wind carried us into the evening air, across the Mississippi River and up the length of Illinois, where we made a wide arc over Lake Michigan, up State Street, veering left, right, under, then over the elevated trains, past Wimpy's hamburger restaurant, and straight through the front door of the Museum of Science and Industry. Once inside, we circled the neck of a brontosaurus, flew through the open jaws of a Tyrannosaurus rex, and dove headlong into the shaft of the coal-mine exhibition. On the way home, we swung by a restaurant where Sally Rand sat eating a steak and drinking a glass of beer. Rising through the clouds, we headed back home.

"Who is Sally Rand?" I asked.

"A story for another time," he said. "Now let's go to sleep."

My father was bone thin, his hair nearly black. His face clean-shaven, symmetrical, serious, open, friendly, and formal—with an ironic gleam at the edge of one eye few photographers failed to capture. His smooth skin turned chestnut each summer but never seemed to burn, as if he could go on absorbing light forever. Long loose hands, neatly pared nails, knobby knees, and beautiful, nearly perfect slender feet. I remember his body in sections, never having seen my father naked—in the altogether, as the saying goes.

I try to remember his walk, how he crossed a room and lowered himself into a chair, how he reached for a book from the shelf. I think of a black-and-white snapshot of him lifting me as a toddler, extending his arms so that I could place the star on top of the Christmas tree. I imagine how he caught a baseball, leapt, tagged the man out at first base, stood up, wiped his brow with his sleeve, put his cap back on, crouched, hands on his knees, and waited for the next batter. In one of my early memories, I am four years old, running behind my father's car as it pulls away down the crushed-gravel drive, raising clouds of chalk-white dust. In another, I am seven or eight, waiting for my dad to come home because we're going to a father-son and -daughter picnic supper at my school. I stand in the sleeping porch off my bedroom listening for his car. Finally, my mother comes in to tell me that he's not coming. He probably forgot. And so the inconsolable grief and father-longing I will carry the rest of my life constellates in my heart.

Try as I might, I cannot retrieve memories of my father in good health. By the 1960s, more often than not, I woke up in the morning to the sound of him gagging, coughing, and throwing up in the bathroom at my end of the hall in order to keep my mother and sister from hearing. Gaunt, pale, hungover, and trembling, he would put on a freshly starched white shirt, a conservative necktie, a gray suit and felt fedora, both showing signs of wear, then drive downtown, sit at a rolltop desk, and try to sell lumber at mill price plus two percent cash discount to old friends who weren't buying.

I'm not sure when it first occurred to me that my father even had a body. I suppose I mean my father's body as a man, and that would have been as I entered puberty and became painfully aware of my own body, which was squarish and pudgy in a family of lithe, slender figures. Like many other boys, my attention was drawn to the muscle-building ads at the back of Archie and Superman comic books. My father's body was the very image of the ninety-eight-pound weakling who got sand kicked in his face. My older brother warned me against vitamin supplements—elixirs that grew muscles by magic. Instead, he taught me his football calisthenics, which resulted in stiff, sore muscles that looked exactly the same the next day. Clearly, my body had a mind of its own and went about the business of adolescence oblivious to my wishes.

Meanwhile, my father's body grew weaker and more sickly, his life-force draining out of him and something pulling him in as if he were recoiling from one gut punch after another. Marital troubles, economic woes, his children's health crises and those of his own all contributed to his slow implosion. Throughout my high-school years, he was in and out of hospitals, with emphysema, chronic alcoholism, and suicidal depression.

In my last year of college, I would come home from afternoon classes to find my mother in the kitchen fixing supper. My father would be "lying down" as she put it, which meant he had passed out in their bedroom. It was my job to wake him. I'd step into the darkened room. My father lay faceup as if he were already in a coffin, his jaw slack, mouth hanging open, exhaling a foul chemical breath into the yellowing light. I'd call softly at first, then louder, and when that failed to rouse him, I'd have to touch him, even the thought of which made me shudder.

Ten years later, my father appeared to me a week or so after he died. I had fallen asleep on the bus from Boston to Portland, Maine, returning from his funeral in St. Louis. I felt arms around me, woke with a start, and batted them away. The seat next to me was empty; there was no one in the aisle. Somehow I knew it was my father. Once home, I sank into a grief whose depth surprised me simply because, by the time of his death, I didn't like him very much. We were cordial, on awkward good terms, friendly enough, but cool—wary is more like it. My dad had been one of the town drunks, and I'd had to endure people's sympathy, scorn, the weight of social stigma—and my own shame. Though sober for ten years, he had just plain worn me out. And I kept my distance.

So what was he doing, visiting from an afterlife neither of us believed in? And why was I suddenly so glad to have him around? Let me be clear. When I say he appeared, I don't mean as a spectral form slipping in and out of shadows. No rattling chains or tapping on the tabletop. It was a felt sense in the body, neither scary nor unsettling, which came to feel ordinary and matter-of-fact, often when I faced a tricky decision. For years, I had used my father's reactions as a navigational tool. I gauged the rightness of a decision by the degree of my father's disapproval.

Imagine my surprise when some years later I found myself on the phone asking about the cost of training as a massage therapist. I was surprised because I'd committed myself to carving out time in a busy teaching schedule in order to work on a novella I had started that summer. Even more surprising was that my father's spirit was by my side, egging me on. "Let's do it!" he seemed to say. I wanted to put my hand over the phone and say, "You of all people!" For he was siding with a part of me he had always criticized as reckless and impulsive. Now he seemed to want to come along for the ride, as if we were once again poised to hop on the back of Johnny West Wind.

My father became something of an obsession, a mystery I had to solve. His death had opened a portal between this world and the next. It had also opened a door to my own twelve-step recovery—and, indeed, into my own body, the very body he had taught me to leave. I found that I had to approach his story from a number of different angles, vocabularies, and conceptual frames. Psychopathology was not enough. To get the full picture, I needed something akin to an insect's compound eye.

When I first sat down with the astrologer who later became my teacher, friend, and colleague, she was quick to point to Saturn's opposition to the Sun in my natal chart. It suggested an ongoing tension between my sense of self, as indicated by the Sun in Aries, impulsive, playful, and combative, and the part of my psyche that calls me to duty and responsibility, Saturn, in Libra, whose focus is on relationship, harmony, fairness, and justice. The opposition also indicates a struggle between planning and spontaneity, maturity and age, and brings to mind the relationship between the Senex, or old man archetype, and the puer aeternus, or eternal youth, sometimes called the Flying Boy.

In my father's natal chart, the Sun in Libra is within ten degrees of where Saturn sits in my birth chart. I experienced my father's energy in much the same way that I experience Saturn in my own psyche. We might say that my father stood in the place of Saturn or played the role of Saturn in my outer life as well. Or we could say he embodied and amplified the qualities of Saturn. And so in our relationship we acted out the tension between self and other, discord and harmony, starting a fight and keeping the peace. As I look back, I see how it was this very tension that kept us engaged in a relationship—the aim and purpose of Libra. However unskillful we were, and no matter how often or far we fled, we kept coming back; indeed, my father made it clear even after he died that he was still very much involved in my learning to hold the tensions between these psychic poles.

I picture Saturn as an old Yankee farmer, guiding a plow through stony soil, stopping to remove rocks and carry them one by one to add to the stone fence that separates one field from another. Saturn is patient, determined, methodical, and seemingly joyless. Which of course is not the whole story. Like any archetype, Saturn is multifaceted. Saturn acts as a counterweight to other parts of the psyche that want to float or fly away, parts of ourselves that can't seem to make up their minds and go on dithering with no end in sight. Saturn almost always has an end in mind. Saturn energy is not only useful, it is essential. Without it, we'd get nothing done at all. Rigorous and exacting, Saturn asks what it is we really want, and what we're willing to do to get it. On a good day, it's a call to do what is necessary to be in integrity. On a bad day, it sounds like harsh and unending criticism.

And so it was with my father's persistent corrections of our grammar at the dinner table. Meant to educate, they managed instead to dampen our spirits until we all sat eating in stony silence, afraid to utter a word. Like Saturn, my father was a taskmaster, a weighty dark presence, strict about homework. He was the eldest of three children, which no doubt informed his sense of responsibility to instruct, protect, and monitor the behavior of his younger siblings. As an idealist, he sought to re-create his own strict, well-ordered, mostly happy childhood. His allegiance was to an earlier time, and he came to be more and more at odds with the latter half of the twentieth century. By the late 1960s, he was dangerously out of sync and out of touch with the world around him.

Our conflict was fueled, in part, by our similarities. I suspect he saw in me a younger, freer version of himself that he may have envied but also felt was his duty to curtail—for my own good. Something in his own nature he kept struggling to bring under control. I like to believe that I never lost sight of his wild essence, a thread that connected us, however thin it became. But I was busy with rebellion, standing against him on principle and too preoccupied with my own crisis-ridden adolescence to have any sense of my father's inner struggle. Even so, I suspect I was picking up signals, distress signals to be sure, but also signs of life from a darkened ship in thick fog, using the very senses he had forced me to sharpen when I was younger.

Fathers and sons in preindustrial communities worked alongside one another. Whether it was planting, harvesting, sheering sheep, or cutting, framing, and joining timbers, in that slow, fully embodied work, men received something of their father's inherent character and essence through physical proximity, the energy that passes between men's bodies as they walk in a forest or keep watch, their gaze trained on the horizon—an exchange that all but disappeared once fathers and sons were sent into factories and put in service to machines.

When I was five or six years old, we went to a summer camp my sisters attended in Wisconsin. After the season ended, the owners opened the cabins to some of the girls' families. It was a place my father knew from the 1920s, when he'd attended a boys' camp at the same site. A family friend used to say it was the only place she ever saw my father relax. On the lake, he was free of the hay fever he suffered from each year in St. Louis. Here he could draw a fuller breath, and it was here he had swum and played ball with his friends and learned to sail and fish as a boy.

It was the farthest north I'd ever been. We drove for three days, spent two nights in motels with swimming pools whose underwater lights made them glow bright blue in the dark. At last we arrived in a place with cabins and trees that smelled like Christmas, on a lake with an island in the middle that my sister Ann could swim out to and back. I was free to roam here and there, following paths that seem to go on and on into the forest and yet looped back to the safety of the campground. The night was darker here than I'd ever seen it. At dusk, we sometimes sat on logs around a fire, and my father told ghost stories. I loved this place. My whole body changed, opened, and somehow expanded. And so did my father's. I don't know how I knew that, but I did. It's as if we tuned in to each other even from distances during the day and in our sleep from different rooms. I was coming alive to something outside the only world I'd known. Even then, I knew I wanted to live in this northern world of cool shadows, where live things sounded at night in trees and across the lake—loons they were called, and their maniacal laughter was terrifying and exciting. Something deep in my nature was fed and enlivened by the lake, the loons, the cool, darkened pathways through the woods, and it set some internal compass toward the north—first to Maine and later to British Columbia.

My father got sober in 1975. Though putting down the drink certainly made a difference, many felt it was too late. Emphysema had already taken hold of him, the damage was done, he was dying. I saw it differently. While it was true he struggled for breath, he was lighter somehow. A great weight had been lifted out of his heart and mind. I graduated from Webster University just as my dad was released from rehab, and I left for France in September for my first teaching job. My parents visited me the following spring. We spent a few days in Paris before traveling north so they could see where I worked. I remember my dad's surprise and delight when he realized that dogs in France understood French. He walked more slowly, had less energy, and had difficulty breathing. I felt impatient and embarrassed by my frumpy Midwestern parents who threatened to undermine the worldly sophistication I was trying hard to cultivate. But when I turned around, waiting for them to catch up, I saw my father looking at everything, taking it all in. I'd been in France for eight months and in many ways took Paris for granted. And there was my father looking around in an amazement I'd remembered feeling but had lost. He hadn't been in Europe since before the war. I suspect he was letting his memories show themselves before they were joined by the fresh impressions he was forming in the present. I realized he'd had a life before he was my father—a full one—and parts of his history were quietly unfolding in his mind, even as I was remembering my own sense of astonishment on seeing Paris for the first time a few years earlier.

I didn't see much of my father in the last decade of his life. When I returned to the States in January 1978, I lived with my parents for six months while I applied to graduate programs in American literature, which began in the fall. My dad was sober, and I was still drinking, discreetly, for fear of jeopardizing my father's sobriety, though it was, of course, more to keep my own drinking out of view. My dad was much more at ease. He and my mother were no longer at each other's throats. My mother was less reactive, less afraid. My father, less defensive. Remembering my high-school years, I remained guarded. Until I too began to soften. Whatever was different in my father was making a difference in me. We talked about the graduate programs I was applying to, my interest in the emergence of American literature and our national character. We talked about the transcendentalists' roots in German Romanticism and Ralph Waldo Emerson's 1837 address to the students of Harvard, often considered to be America's intellectual declaration of independence. We talked about Mark Twain and the wisdom or folly of writing in dialect, the pedagogy of William James and John Dewey. He described his own graduate seminars at the University of Chicago in the 1930s, self-governing groups under the direction and guidance of a professor who acted more as a process facilitator than merely a content expert—and the fistfights between Communist and Fascist students in the hallways.

We were rediscovering our common ground—literature, storytelling, and the principles of progressive education—a territory much larger than either of us imagined, as if, while walking through the woods, we had come upon a large open meadow. We were learning to trust each other, certainly, but just as important, we were coming to trust the earth under our feet.

Puer energy is slippery, elusive, forever taking flight, always just out of reach. Idealized. Beloved by the Greeks, who depicted him as lithe, youthful, androgynous, and athletic. To these traits, psychologist and philosopher James Hillman adds "narcissistic, inspired, effeminate, phallic, inquisitive, pensive, passive, fiery, and capricious." He goes on to argue that the Puer (or Puella in a woman) is an essential part of the psyche and must be considered in relation to the Senex/old man (or Seneca/old woman) archetype. We need to develop both in order to grow toward wholeness. For they work in concert, sparking, stretching, and balancing each other. With too much Puer/Puella, we shirk responsibility and regress to adolescent impulse, whim, and fantasy. We lose touch with consensus reality and become ungrounded, ignoring Daedalus's warning to his son Icarus not to fly too close to Helios. Not enough Puer/Puella, and we lose touch with imagination and our capacity to dream, to soar, and to surrender to creative flow. We lose contact with spontaneous enthusiasm, without which nothing much gets done.

Not enough Senex/Seneca, and nothing gets done at all. We lose focus, direction, and a sense of purpose. We forget why we embarked on a course of action in the first place, forget important lessons of history, disregard the ancestors, and throw away the structures necessary to give ritual its transformative power, charging ahead ever more recklessly into certain catastrophe, with Senex and Saturn cringing as they look on in horror.

My father stood in the role of Senex/Saturn; as my father, it was his responsibility, and I suspect he was particularly harsh because he was at odds with his own untamed and evasive Puer energy. My duty as his son was to keep that wildness alive and to express it, pushing back against what I saw as constraints, even tyranny. The challenge here of course is to modulate the wildness without killing it. An art we have mostly forgotten in parenting and every other aspect of our lives. Luckily, Sophia (wisdom), anima mundi (world soul), and the divine imagination find ways of doing the work we tend to neglect, and I was drawn to any number of people, men and women, with strong Senex/Crone/Saturn energy to temper my Puer and make it more workable. And in my thirty years in college classrooms and public workshops, I encountered any number of Puer/Puella students who called me again and again to step into the role of Senex/Saturn as their guide and mentor.

"Your dad should have been a teacher," his brother told me in 1990. "Don't get me wrong," he said, "he was a good lumberman, but his heart was never in it. His heart was in teaching." He "succumbed to the age-old problem," as my uncle put it. You can't raise a family on a teacher's salary. He meant, of course, "and maintain a certain standard of living." I'd heard the story many times—but never from my father directly. Whatever his reasons, my father decided to get married, left graduate school, and entered the family business, which, in the end, failed, along with almost every other wholesale lumber company in the United States after the war.

In a sense, we could say I lived my father's unlived life as a teacher, a life he didn't feel able to choose. I didn't do it for him but because it was in me to live it, one of the vehicles that carried me deeper into my own life. For my dad, it was the crucible of the family that proved to be his transforming agent. Setting aside my opinion of his reasons, there was nothing wrong with my father's choice to enter the family business. What was wrong—or what was missing—was his heart. It was elsewhere. So he tried, in many ways valiantly, to live a life he couldn't love until he did, a life he often felt was not worth living. And yet it was. I used to think that my father's gift to me was showing me the cost of not living your true life. But I suspect his real gift had something to do with the work required to reclaim one's lost heart, taking a turn in the road, however late, that leads back to the center, that follows the pulse back to its source.

Often when I leave the studio, I head into the large second-growth rain forest of Stanley Park instead of walking straight home. I follow a path that leads to a point overlooking Burrard Inlet. A turn in the trail about halfway there brought me up short one day. All of a sudden, I stood looking through two birch trees not at English Bay but at the Wisconsin lake we'd visited when I was very young, the place that brought my father and me alive to each other in a way my body now remembered, as if I were viewing the scene through his eyes, and the sudden upsurge in pleasure in my body also belonged to him. I breathed in the scent of cedar and rotting leaves, remembered my father's emphysema, and realized that my father, unencumbered by lungs, had become breath. Spirit. Wind. Resuming our walk, my father and I continued on toward the Hollow Tree and up to Prospect Point in a silence that often descends between hikers and pilgrims.

On Not Being Southern

When I was seven, my mother took me to meet my Southern cousins. We flew on a prop plane from St. Louis to Richmond, Virginia. My aunt and two cousins met us at the airport. The cousin who was my age, looked at his mother and said, "Is he a damn Yankee?"

I looked at my mother and said, "What's a damn Yankee?"

And so my relationship with the American South began.

I knew enough to know I was not a Southerner. We identified as Midwesterners. Though we used a plural form of "you," we always said it in two distinct syllables: "you all" and never, ever "y'all." True, my parents tended to serve more bourbon than scotch at parties, but most of the men drank the beer brewed by either Mr. Busch (Budweiser) or the Griesedieck Brothers (Falstaff).

Also true that, like our Southern cousins, we knew never to drink gin and tonic in the winter or to wear white after Labor Day. We knew what dance cards were, and girls knew how to unbutton their white kid gloves when they wanted to smoke. We understood that girls from certain families made their debuts, and others did not.

When it came to race relations, things got a little murkier.

Though Missouri entered the Union as a slave state in 1820, we were told that no one on either side of the family tree had ever owned slaves, and everyone had fought in the Union not the Confederate Army during the Civil War. Not that we were exactly freedom fighters. It meant we were that northward-tending, Midwestern kind of prejudiced.

Not Southern.

Though we used "Jew" as a verb, my father said he had many associates of the Jewish faith whom he respected. However, there was a difference between a Jew and a kike, a distinction, he insisted, they made themselves.

The Ku Klux Klan was just plain wrong.

I believe my father loved the South, though he had an odd way of showing it. He would tell stories about Arkansas in dialect, and sometimes sing old songs from—I hang my head in shame—minstrel shows. He had committed a number of the comedy routines of Two Black Crows to memory, and he thought Amos 'n' Andy was about the funniest thing ever.

Two of his best friends lived in Gurdon, Arkansas, and his business often took him to Mississippi and Louisiana, from which he would cart home boxes of pralines. He loved grits, almost anything fried, and corn bread.

Meanwhile I was determined to become a Yankee and fixed my gaze steadily to the north—Chicago was about as far north as I could imagine at first, but as I learned more about geography, I found out there was all kinds of land north of Chicago, Canada even.

In the winter I longed for snow. In the summer, I dreamed about the northern lights. I realized I would have to wait to go to someplace like New York City or, even better, New England, where the real Yankees lived.

And in fact, I ended up in Maine.

But the South does not give up easily. I entered my first collection of short stories in two competitions, and it won one of them. The Southern one. As proud as I was, I kept wishing I'd won the one in Iowa. Even though not one of my stories was set in the South—remember, cousins, St. Louis ain't the South—and even though I had settled in northern New England, I began to be associated with Southern writers. To make matters worse, I was accepted for a residency at the Virginia Center for the Creative Arts, right across the road from the all girls' college my mother had wanted to attend but could not because of the Depression.

I drove down in an old Volvo with Maine license plates, and I feared for my life. Here I was all Yankee-identified, with long hair and old leftist tendencies—at an artist colony, no less. Not all that far up the road from Lynchburg, where Jerry Falwell preached. I felt myself to be in some kind of incomprehensible trouble and didn't sleep well for a number of weeks. People joked about my fears. "You don't have to worry until they actually light the cross. That's when you start running."

Then I found myself in a group that included a truly crazy writer from southern Mississippi and a Jewish woman who'd been raised in the South—laughing. I mean we laughed hard at every meal, so hard that people at other tables were annoyed with us. Disruptive laughter. Laughter on the verge of tears. And then it occurred to us. There was a terrible grief in it. A grief about the vast gulf that still existed between North and South—even in the 1990s, even among artists and writers.

When I'd tell my fellow writers about my uneasiness about being in the South, they'd counter with stories of how they'd been humiliated at Harvard and New York University for their accents, for ideas they didn't even hold to but were assumed to have. They spoke about the jaundiced view of Southerners held by people who only know the South through The New Yorker or the Chicago Tribune. People who in fact don't know the South at all.

The pain I felt was due to the split in my own heart. I was raised in a city that divided North from South along Delmar Boulevard, as surely as the Mason-Dixon Line had separated the Union and the Confederacy.

I had spent most of my life fleeing to the North, where I never really felt I belonged. I think of the time in Boston when I overheard two Black women up from the South, speaking to each other on a bus, and I started to weep. I hadn't heard such beautiful English in years.

Memory. That other mother tongue.

The Soul, Herself Surprised

There's a story told in Sufi circles that goes something like this: God summons the soul of Adam to show him what he has in mind for the human being, a kind of prototype. Adam's soul recoils in horror. "Me?" he cries. "In that little clay pot? No way!" So God sets the choirs of angels to singing. Adam's soul swoons in ecstasy . . . And the next thing Adam knows, he wakes up in a human body.

I've always been partial to the idea that God had to trick us to get us here, having myself often felt if not exactly betrayed, misled somehow, certainly let down, and often disappointed by life on earth. My soul feels constrained and cramped—the pace too slow, the atmosphere dense, the weather inconsistent: one moment cold and icy, the next hot, humid, and full of mosquitoes.

One thing is for sure: The soul remembers where she came from.

But what is this entity, this phenomenon we call "soul"? This wonder that animates the body, lives on after the body dies, and which many claim comes around again and again in different incarnations, something that can be lost—and retrieved—split apart and made whole again, which may or may not be subject to eternal damnation and is made conspicuous by its absence. I believe it was Hazrat Inayat Khan who said that once the soul leaves, the body loses all its charm.

The Greeks tell another story about the soul, who is called Psyche and is so beautiful that Aphrodite, the goddess of love and a great beauty in her own right, becomes jealous and sends her son, Eros, to make sure Psyche falls in love with a monster. But Eros himself falls in love with Psyche and takes her to a heavenly palace where he makes her promise never to look on his face. She begins to miss her sisters and asks Eros if they might visit. He agrees, as long as she doesn't take any advice they may give her. You know how it is with elder sisters. They manage to convince Psyche that her husband is the monster she was prophesied to marry and should be murdered, so Psyche approaches him one night as he sleeps, lifts the lamp, and sees his beauty. A drop of hot oil falls on his shoulder. He wakes up, realizes that Psyche has betrayed him, and flees. When no one else dares to help Psyche find Eros, she turns to his mother, Aphrodite, who is furious and decides to teach them both a lesson. She gives Psyche a number of impossible tasks, and in each case, Psyche gets help from the natural and supernatural realms, which only makes Aphrodite madder, so she decides to send Psyche to fetch a box of beauty secrets from Persephone, the queen of the underworld. Psyche must under no condition look into the box. Once again, with help from other realms, Psyche figures out how to enter the underworld without dying, gets the box, and has very nearly completed this the most difficult task when she pauses. If what is in the box will enhance the beauty of a goddess, just think what it might do for a mere mortal such as herself. You already guessed. She opens the box and falls into a deathlike sleep. Meanwhile, Eros, having recovered from his wounded pride, realizes he cannot live without Psyche, rushes to revive her, and then pleads his case to Zeus, who sorts it out with Aphrodite and hands Psyche a cup of ambrosia that makes her immortal, and Psyche and Eros are reunited—forever.

Another thing seems certain: The soul learns everything the hard way—by experience and through repetition.

Many poets and metaphysicians describe the downward motion of the soul. It descends, has weight. It has "bandaged moments" when it is "too appalled to stir," has agency, "selects her own Society/Then shuts the door" or "rolls across the floor like a bomb," as Emily Dickinson reminds us. The soul is dangerous. It wanders, gets lost, finds its way home, then sets off again. The soul is restless, yet seems subject to a gravity all its own. "Soul is vulnerable and suffers," writes James Hillman, "it is passive and remembers." Passive or not, the soul is persistent in getting our attention in any way she can and seems to have the capacity to intercede and redirect, exerting a tidal pull as compelling as the moon's. And like the moon, the soul seems to wax and wane, though it is my awareness of her that fluctuates. I may lose sight of her, but she never loses sight of me. She comes to mind as thought or image, occurs in the body as a notion, hunch, inkling, or symptom. She makes her way by going, and knows where she is once she gets there.

"See? This is what I meant all along," she says.

"Then why didn't you say so?" I cry.

"Oh but I did," she replies. "Look at your dreams, your depressions, your medical records, and your divorces."

The soul proceeds obliquely, by association, following tangents and digressions. She bids us turn this way, then that, without explanation and for reasons that only become clear later—if ever. Mythology, fairy tales, and folklore are all full of sudden reversals of fortune, and as children we delight in them until we ourselves are lost in the dark woods, sure we have followed the directions we left home with, and yet there was no mention of the place where we now stand, no mention at all of the five divergent paths before us, none of which seems like the right one. We become immobilized, and then remember the troll under the bridge, whose advice we ignored. Often as not at this point in the story, we fall into a deep sleep, and something else takes over; ants, an eagle, elves, angels, and ancestors set to work to get the impossible job done so we can be on our way. Planets align. Vectors converge. A portal opens. We wake up in the same place, but the light has changed. The air carries the scent of sweet grass or wild roses. And somehow, we know which next step is the right one—for now.

Looking back, I often see how unrelated events began to form a shape or pattern. A road trip. Two dreams. A love affair. A cancellation. Three chance meetings. Easter Vigil. A conversion.

It's August. I'm driving home from New Mexico to Maine. One night I dream I'm heading north through Vermont toward the Canadian border. I know this is an indirect route. A few nights later, I have the same dream, but at the moment I imagine I am taking a scenic detour, the dream itself says, "No, you are going home, and home is across the border."

Had I not fallen in love with James, I might never have become a Catholic. Had we not broken up, I might never have attended a conference in Quebec City where I met people who pointed me toward Vancouver. And had I not met a poet on Peaks Island some twenty years earlier, I might never have spent eight summers in New Mexico and never dreamed the dreams, while driving back to Maine, that I was, in fact, heading home to Canada . . . six years before I moved there.

The soul is drawn to specific places. At first northern New Mexico seemed like alien territory. The high desert was unlike any place I had ever lived or visited, barren blown earth that stretched in every direction. I arrived by train in December. After a few days, once my eyes had adjusted to the light, I discovered a wide range of colors in what at first seemed only brown or yellow ocher. Then there was the sky—bigger than I could have ever imagined. My response was visceral. Something in the blood, the heart said: Yes. I felt my imagination unfold and expand. My soul sensed a freedom she'd never known before—or at least not for a very long time. And so in the summers between 1995 and 2002, I worked on the stories and novellas that were included in my second collection.

By contrast, Leningrad felt familiar from the moment I arrived, maybe because of its human scale. And yet it had an unreal, dreamlike quality. It was March, cold and dank, the sidewalks full of dirty snow. The butter-cream yellow, robin's-egg blue, and dark red of its buildings vibrated against the flat gray of the Baltic sky. I returned the next summer for a course in Russian. Walking through a park one day, I was suddenly overcome with fatigue. Energy drained out of my body and into the earth. I felt pulled down. All I knew was that I had to keep going and find my way out of this park. Later, I learned that it had been created over a mass grave of people who died during the siege of Leningrad. A psychic once told me I had decided to reincarnate immediately after the war. Whether or not I had walked over my bodily remains from a previous life, one of the things that compelled me to return to Russia was grief. Having been raised in a culture that did its best to deny grief altogether, I needed to find someplace on earth where my own considerable grief was reflected in language, painting, music, and liturgy that expressed something like the full depth and scope of it.

The soul is drawn to specific people—soul mates, soul friends, soul families. "Lovers don't finally meet somewhere. They're in each other all along," says Rumi, a line that is often read at weddings. And it's true, soul mates do sometimes end up happily married, and even to each other, but it's not always that simple. My friend Sarah, after a marriage and a number of love affairs, discovered that her soul mate was not, in fact, in human form during her current incarnation, which meant she could stop worrying about it and get on with her soul's work in this lifetime. John O'Donohue talks about the soul friend or Anam Cara, a term he traces to the first Irish monastic communities, but the kind of relationship he describes goes back to the desert mothers and fathers and has influenced contemporary forms of soul accompaniment and certainly predates the Christian era. New Agers talk about soul families, souls that decide to incarnate around the same time, though not necessarily in the same geographic location, and meet up at some point for purposes of healing, releasing, supporting, challenging, or wounding (yes, that too). Caroline Myss talks about soul contracts that need to be completed and dissolved for the benefit of everyone.

All of this is tricky to work out, given that we tend to forget our pre-incarnational agreements the moment we're born (or certainly within the first year)—and then remember, slowly, reluctantly, often doubting they ever existed. And who knows? I try to keep an open mind. It can also be tricky given the emotional intensity involved. I find it tough to discern how much or little the soul is involved in love affairs. At work here is a tendency to idealize the beloved and to hope against hope that they, at last, are the one and only—no more searching and pining away. That something out of the ordinary is happening is clear. The pulse quickens. The heart races. A great deal is stirring in my depths, fired by my imagination and active dreaming states. Very nearly every figure in the unconscious is called to action and stands at the ready. A felt sense of connection and kinship, yet something wonderfully strange and compelling . . . all pointing to activities of the soul. And then there's the question of compatibility, which is, well, assumed until the drug wears off and those figures in the unconscious remember their old injuries and seek reparation or revenge.

More often than not, a meeting with a member of our soul family is charged with erotic energy. Intense, unmistakable, and impossible to ignore, the experience calls us to the bedroom, thinking surely this is the domestic bliss we have longed for and which is lacking in our present circumstance. We are either quick or slow to inform our spouse of the new development, and almost before we know it, the moving van is rolling us toward happily-ever-after. Of course there are things to work out, details, divorce papers to be filed, real estate to liquidate or relinquish, lawyers to hire—oh and custody of the children, all of which can be sorted out later. What matters most is that we have found each other and are together—again—at last. And yet it seems we have not yet finished unloading the furniture when distressing signals of discord arise, and, you can fill in your own particulars. True, it sometimes works out amicably, but all too often it's the wrong form to begin with. Misreading the signals, we want to domesticate what is meant to remain wild. Something about soul family connections threatens Hestia, hearth, and home. These relationships call for the wisdom of Sophia to guide them with intelligence, discernment, and any number of other qualities that call to be developed. They insist on their own territory, their own space, and it often wants to be large—if not vast—to work themselves out in.

Whether or not James and I were soul mates or soul family, our love affair brought me slap-up against pressing life questions—its emerging purpose, its work, and the kind of soil it needed in order to take root. A call was involved, and I needed to be free to answer—but first I had to be able to hear the call. By the time I met James, I was spending long weekends and any other blocks of time I could manage in Quebec City to work on a novella, which kept coming to me in dreamlike states when I was there. It felt as if the central character was guiding me through the city, showing me the orphanage she had escaped from, the brothel she'd been led to in a dream and the prostitutes who took her in and gave her shelter and training, the art school where she modeled and first encountered the ideas of Les

Automatistes, an art movement that was to change her life and alter the history of Quebec. As I wrote in cafés, in libraries, and at my desk at home in Maine, the Fates were at work on other projects.

I was spending more and more time in New York City with James. He had been asked by a musician colleague to help with Easter Vigil mass in New Jersey, so I drove down to meet him and then we'd spend the following week in New York. Almost from the moment I took my place among the parishioners standing outside as the priest built the fire and prepared the Paschal candle, I sensed that I had entered a powerful ritual space, the likes of which I had never encountered in a Christian context, a space not altogether of this world, and yet which felt deeply rooted in the truth of earlier earth-based traditions. As we tilted our individual candles toward one another to receive the flame from the original fire and followed the priest through the doors and into the dark, empty womb of the church, I sensed the accompanying spirits of the precolonial world, who were not there to be converted or changed in any way, but who were summoned by what came to be known as the unity of the Holy Spirit, which neither dismisses nor demeans the wisdom that preceded her, indeed, out of which she evolved.

It was as if I knew the ritual, remembered it, some part of me recognized the taproot of the whole Abrahamic line. My soul knew she was coming home, not to a political institution or set of dogmas but to the heart and essence of teachings that the earliest communities of Jews and Gentiles followed in their many forms and expressions long before the First Council of Nicaea. My soul was coming home to herself.

In 2004, Massachusetts legalized same-sex marriage, and couples from all over New England and beyond flocked to the state to get a marriage license. As a notary public in Maine, I had officiated four weddings by then and was asked by gay friends in Connecticut, who'd gotten their legal documents in Massachusetts, if I would help them create a ceremony for friends and family at their home. So marriage was in the air that autumn as James and I were coming apart, and neither of us wanted to admit it. I had joined a men's meditation group that met on Sunday evenings, and during one meditation I saw a ring, gold and silver in a Celtic weave. The image was so clear that the next day I visited a friend's curio shop and asked if she'd ever seen anything that came close. She opened a drawer, rummaged around, pulled out a ring, and said, "Like this?" "That's it!" I said. It fit, so I bought it. I knew it was a wedding ring—my wedding ring—and the marriage was an inner one, the coniunctio, or alchemical marriage, a union of opposites. The one friend I knew would understand was a Celtic Christian, mystic, and massage therapist. Together we designed a ritual of completion and opening, honoring and invoking my ancestors and spirit guides, releasing what was no longer alive in me, healing what had been wounded, making a vow and a promise, and then receiving a final blessing. Like most newlyweds, I had little understanding of what I'd gotten myself into, for there were stages of purification, chaos, darkness, putrefaction, burning, psychic deaths, and awakenings yet to come.

Years later, when I told the story to a friend in Vancouver, he said, "So, you're married to Jesus?"

"Not exactly." I smiled. "It feels more like Sophia, wisdom, the soul of the world."

My Mother, Remembering

My mother could never remember whether or not she had met Gertrude Stein. She remembered her coming to St. Louis to speak at the Wednesday Club some time after the war, and she seemed to recall eating a Waldorf salad, but as to Stein and what she said, my mother drew a blank.

If she attended the lecture that day, it was because Gertrude Stein lived in Paris, and my mother loved all things Parisian, but not the way the Métro smelled like garlic. She preferred the look of Paris to its smell. She liked how it felt to be walking along a boulevard in open-toed high-heeled shoes with ankle straps and her good wool coat with the fur collar. She didn't like small furry animals when they were alive but didn't mind them dead around her neck. Later in life, she wore a fox stole with its head and tail and claws. She liked that very much.

She used to tell me I was smart like a fox.

"Like the ones you used to wear around your neck?" I asked.

"Oh no," she said. "Not those. The ones who got away."

She spent the fall, winter, and spring of 1932–1933 in Paris at Madame Bouyer's Study Home for Young Ladies. To practice her French, she kept a diary, the only one she ever wrote. In her round, left-handed cursive, she kept a careful record of museums visited, with whom, where they dined, and what they ate. She described the other girls in the house—from Chicago, Baltimore, Memphis—and the clothes they bought from Galeries Lafayette or Printemps. Simple descriptions in language that was useful—nothing too speculative or interior—in one of three tenses: the simple past, the present continuous, and the going to future.

My mother lived a thoroughly unexamined life, and she'd have been the first to tell Plato to his face that it was well worth living.

Every moment of it.

She loved *La Bohème* at the Paris Opera and how they made

it snow onstage in act III, and was delighted when, after the final curtain, she and her escort, a boy from Wisconsin, discovered it was snowing outside. She was glad she'd worn her good wool coat with the fur collar, but she wished she'd worn more sensible shoes. Her escort held his overcoat above their heads, and they ran across the Place de l'Opéra to catch a taxi.

She didn't wear a hat.

She didn't like hats.

She remembered some Russian stirring up trouble that spring, though she wrote nothing about it in her diary, and later couldn't recall what it was all about. So many, she said, were stirring up trouble in Paris in those days. The ship sailing home passed another ship leaving New York Harbor with no lights or horns or fanfare of any kind, which was very odd. The ship was silent and dark, as if it were full of ghosts. Later she learned it was a German passenger ship, and once the war began it made more sense.

Many years later, her children grown, she sat drinking bourbon and listening to 78 rpm recordings of Caruso late into the night, thinking of her time in Paris, when the present continuous had been so interesting and the going to future so full of promise.

My mother was born six weeks after the assassination of Archduke Ferdinand in Sarajevo, which started the First World War. She grew up in a brick house on Cates Avenue, six blocks north of Delmar, an easy walk to Moll's market, whose barbeque sauce was made famous by a colleague of her cousin Patty, who became the first woman vice president of an advertising agency in St. Louis, which I only found out years later when I met her myself.

For some reason my mother never much liked Patty, who after she graduated from college, joined the navy. As a lieutenant, she trained officers and carried secret orders on the train up and down the East Coast and by plane to California. Toward the end of her life, Patty showed me wartime photos and told me stories about the young men and women pictured in them—where each photo was taken, what they had eaten at picnics, who was in love with whom.

She carried top-secret orders for the Potsdam Conference and for Okinawa.

"What about Hiroshima and Nagasaki?" I asked.

"I don't remember," said Patty. "We were trained to forget."

The house on Cates Avenue had a bay window. The piano was there, so they called that the music room. The living room was across the entrance hall, and a bit farther down was a lavatory for guests. The dining room, pantry, and kitchen were at the back of the house. The upstairs bedrooms at the front of the house belonged to her mother and her younger sister, Carol. My mother and her father had the back bedrooms. There was a full bath on the second floor. On the third floor were a few finished rooms and a bath for the maid, Freda, one of those wonderful German girls who came up to St. Louis from the farm to go into service, as it was then called.

My mother took her first steps beside an iris bed at the front of the house, her father's left hand at the ready to grab if she wobbled. In his right hand, a cigar. When she was six, she played an angel in the Christmas play. "I knew I was an angel," she said, "but my mother wasn't so sure." She told the shepherds not to be afraid of her and then sang a lullaby, presumably for the baby Jesus and not the shepherds who were expected to stay awake. At Mahler's Dancing Academy, she took classes in comportment and singing lessons at Alice Whitney Conant's Enright Avenue studio, which offered tea recitals Saturday afternoons at three o'clock.

She was fifth in her class one year at Rossman School, and by May she had risen to fourth. There was a little Boston bulldog called Snipper, the only dog they ever owned, and her thirteenth birthday party at summer camp in Wisconsin. There was Sunday school at Pilgrim Congregational Church. Sometimes at the weekend, they'd go to Pflager Farms on the bluffs of the Mississippi River, where peacocks wandered the grounds and there were ponies, though she never much liked riding. She preferred swimming and canoeing. A gorgeous house. The Pflagers were friends of her parents, and when they died, Mrs. Wells bought the property and made a fat farm out of it, where people can go when they want to lose weight.

In the Saint Louis Art Museum was a huge painting of the French Revolution, not the one with the woman's breast falling out of her bodice, another one, but every bit as full of blood and glory in colors so bright you could almost hear the muskets firing. Generally speaking, she preferred the quiet landscapes of Constable to the turbulent seascapes of Turner. She loved Renoir and the impressionists, was less enthusiastic about van Gogh and Gauguin, and simply could not abide Max Beckmann. As for the Americans, it was Missouri's own Thomas Hart Benton and the Wyeths in New England.

Her first evening dress was silk and tulle and she wore it to the Fortnightly Dance at the Country Club, where girls stood to one side of the room and waited for boys to approach and ask them to dance, each writing the other's name with a golf pencil on a dance card, so everyone knew which dance was with whom. Things didn't always go smoothly, and one of the matronly chaperones would have to take things in hand, literally, grabbing a shy or reluctant boy by the arm and marching him across the floor to claim one of the wallflowers who were now even more mortified than they had been a moment earlier. Somehow, her friend Suzanna managed to disappear into the powder room to read a section of The Brothers Karamazov, which she had carefully cut from the paperback edition so it would fit into her beaded bag. There she spent the evening in a stall, reading and dreaming of Vassar College where she would one day find relief.

As a girl, my mother studied voice with Helen Traubel, who later moved to New York and pursued a career as a concert and opera singer. President Harry Truman engaged her to coach his daughter. "She had about as much luck with Margaret Truman as she had with me," said my mother. "But I had the good sense not to insist on singing at Carnegie Hall." This probably was not Truman's idea, but his wife's mother, who never approved of Harry and thought Bess had married beneath her. While living with them at the White House, she used to turn to her daughter and ask if Mr. Truman would be joining them for supper that evening. "Imagine!" said my mother. "Poor old Harry Truman."

She didn't think much of Truman's policies—he was a Democrat—but she liked it that he dropped an atom bomb on Nagasaki on her thirty-fifth birthday.

She liked to tell us about her great-great-grandfather whom the Religious Society of Friends disowned, not for marrying a non-Quaker but for refusing to apologize. Here she would raise her chin in glad defiance, as if to say: This is the stuff I am made of. She also liked telling us about the day her mother had come to Mary Institute for a parent-teacher conference and was standing in the front hall with the headmaster, who, as the students poured into the corridors to change classes, said, "Who is that awful girl wearing all that lipstick?"

"That," said my grandmother, "is my daughter, Betty."

By all accounts, my maternal grandmother, Jesse Smith, was strict and exacting. She was a stickler for punctuality with a fondness for the quarter hour. Dinner was at 6:15. And if the telephone rang during the meal, Freda would answer, step into the dining room, and before she could say who was on the phone, my grandmother would raise her right hand and repeat the rule: "No telephone calls during dinner. Tell whomever it is to call back after 7:35." My mother and her sister would exchange a sideways glance and go back to eating.

Grandmother Jessie was the daughter of a physician in Springfield, Missouri. Though not wealthy, they were respectable and solidly middle class. She was a college graduate, a Latin scholar, and a voracious reader. In photographs she is almost always shown with a book in hand or within easy reach. She was a snob and my mother's cousin Patty used to say, "Add a silver-headed walking stick, a velvet choker, and she'd have been Mary Queen of Scots." After attending Patty's high-school graduation in a nearby suburb, my grandmother remarked that she was surprised that public-school students had learned to play classical music, a string quartet, no less, and not just the standard fare of marching bands.

My grandmother showed her affection for my mother in assembling photographs in two large albums entitled "The Life of Elizabeth Ferrin Mansfield Until Her Marriage." In her labeling of the photographs she showed a dry, ironic sense of humor. My mother's humor leaned more toward the vaudeville style of Fibber McGee and Molly. Her mother was delighted when she started dating my father, who also read Latin. At last, one of her daughters had a beau she could talk to about things that mattered to her. My mother thought the study of dead languages was silly because nobody spoke them anymore. Latin teaches us grammar and logic, my father argued. My mother wasn't interested in logic. Her line of reasoning was neither linear nor reasonable. One thought. An ellipsis. Another thought. A jump, a sharp turn in midair, and then off in an unexpected direction, which to her made perfect sense but left others scratching their heads. Especially my father.

I was living in Quebec City in the summer of 2003. I called my mother on Bastille Day and sang the first few lines of "La Marseillaise," which she picked up and continued to the end. At eighty-nine, she remembered all three verses in French, but she could never remember how she met my father.

Their wedding, however, she remembered in detail. Lightning struck the church the night before, knocking the organ out of commission. My mother wanted to postpone the wedding, but her mother said, "Over my dead body." A friend of the family happened to be in a string quartet and had his instrument in the car, so my mother walked down the aisle on her father's arm accompanied by a cello.

She could never stand the sound of a cello after that.

"It could have been worse," I said. "He might have had an accordion in his car."

"Or worse, still," she said, "bagpipes!"

My parents made a handsome couple, and their wedding portrait, formal as it was, pulses with life. My mother stands in yards of white satin, a long train gathered in a wave around her feet, as if she'd just risen from the sea foam and been caught by a handsome sailor, still stunned by his good luck. At the end of the Great Depression and on the cusp of another world war, the photograph shines with grace, an assurance of good fortune, and, looking back, the courage and love with which they navigated, however unskillfully, any number of calamities in the years that followed.

My mother was uncommonly photogenic. Hers was a striking beauty, dark and solemn, in any number of formal studio portraits taken in the year she and her sister made their debuts. A few years later, she appeared on the cover of the Sunday supplement as "Bride of the Week," wearing a green-and-white-striped shirtwaist dress, her long skirt spread over the bench she sat on as she gazed into a vase full of white lilies at her feet. In contrast to these portraits, snapshots in those same years and for seventy years after show her with a wide grin that revealed a chip in her left front tooth from when a classmate thumped her head as she drank from the water fountain at school. She never had it capped or did anything to try to hide it. Her smile is genuine and irrepressible aboard a sailboat on Lake Michigan the summer after she returned from France. My father appears at the tiller in another photo, clearly from the same trip, visiting his or her parents at a summer house a few months after they had announced their engagement.

He said he fell in love with her because she looked like an English actress of the time. I suspect my mother was drawn to him not just because he was handsome, personable, and bright, but because he was fun—and so was his family, especially compared to her own strict teetotalling parents. She and her sister used to gargle with perfume before they set foot inside their front door after a night out on the town. "The dime-store variety, not the good stuff from France," my mother was quick to add. And while my father's mother also abstained from alcohol, everybody else in his family liked to take a drink now and again (and again), and her father-in-law-to-be knew the lyrics to almost every drinking song of the 1890s.

When the DePews went to Maine in the summer, my grandfather played the piano for the nondenominational services in the small neighborhood chapel on Sundays. He always said he could play anything—as long as it was in the key of C. Once the more pious among the summer people had left the chapel, he would break into "Beer Barrel Polka," his children and their friends chiming in until it was time for lunch. All of which appealed to my mother's sense of mischief.

She was full of surprises, my mother was, and a natural comedienne. A look in her eye, a facial expression, an offhand remark would send the three of us younger children into gales of laughter—at exactly the wrong moment, in church, for instance. Her social gaffs mortified me when I was a teenager. She seemed unaware that people laughed at her, and didn't care whom she offended or how deeply. When I got older, I noticed she knew exactly what she was doing—I could see her gauging the effect. She enjoyed setting people on edge. A born trickster, she couldn't resist opening the door to the Lord of Misrule from time to time just to see what would happen.

She held unorthodox views on history, theology, social status, and the natural world. French men were generally short in stature because all the tall ones were killed in the Napoleonic Wars; the shorter fellows could duck out of the way of the bullets. Sometimes, she explained, a healthy instinct for survival was mistaken for cowardice. The northern lights were the result of sunbeams bouncing off the North Pole. Race, religion, and politics weren't discussed at the dinner table; they were bad for digestion. Children from old families with money sometimes led debauched and dissolute lives—often in the third generation—because they'd been handed everything on a silver platter and didn't know what to do with themselves. There was nothing wrong with the new moneyed as long as they didn't show off. We ourselves didn't have much money but enjoyed certain privileges and the social standing of those who did because—well—we were descended from respectable hardworking people and knew our place.

The virgin birth was a mistaken notion. Jesus was born to Mary and Joseph in the normal way, which my mother was not prepared to discuss further. She left that to my father, who in turn left it to the progressive schools we attended. While there was nothing inherently wrong with our Catholic neighbors, they talked a good bit of nonsense and were gravely mistaken when it came to the question of birth control. How I was born five and a half years after my sister Carol, who was supposed to be the third and final child in a family of enthusiastic supporters of

Planned Parenthood, remains a mystery. An "afterthought" people explained. I preferred to think of it as a miracle. "Suit yourself," said my mother, "but don't let it go to your head."

Whatever the circumstances of my birth, my mother remembered nothing about it. She'd been given a drug called twilight sleep and went out like a light, which meant I was left to fend for myself, squirming and kicking my way through the tight flesh tunnel until someone grabbed my ankles and pulled me into a very cold, very bright room full of voices all talking at once.

When my brother was born eight years earlier, my mother got out of bed, dressed, packed her overnight bag, and headed toward the elevator. A nurse stopped her and asked where she thought she was going.

"Home," said my mother. "I'm not sick."

"But Mrs. DePew," said the nurse, "you've just had a baby."

She walked my mother back to her room, brought my brother to her, and placed him in her arms. "There now," she said. "You remember."

What my mother may have lacked in maternal sentiment, she made up for in managerial genius. While Mary may have had the better part in the Bible story, had it not been for Martha, Jesus wouldn't have had dinner that day. My father was something of a dreamer and hopeless around the house. My mother's motto was: If you want anything done around here, you have to do it yourself—or hire the right person for the job. And so it was she who called the furnace man and the chimney sweep in the fall; she who engaged the yardman to mow the lawn, rake leaves, and tend the garden; she who cooked and ironed on the weekend and supervised the cook, the cleaner, and the laundress during the week. To all these tasks, she brought a military bearing and precision. She ran a taut ship, which was especially important when the seas got rough, which they did for a number of years.

She had a volatile temper. She could turn on a dime and fly into a rage, sometimes a violent one, and had little or no idea of the damage she caused. Indeed, she seemed as surprised and perplexed by her outbursts as everyone around her. Yet I don't remember her apologizing. More and more cracks appeared in the placid exterior of her postwar suburban life. Right before her eyes my father was disappearing into the vortex of alcoholism, his business failing even as everyone around us seemed to be making money hand over fist. As the 1960s gathered momentum, the world itself seemed to be flying apart.

Ours was a weird friendship. I had an uncanny, intuitive understanding of her dark side. Somehow I had access to her nocturnal consciousness, which confounded both her and my father. This was dangerous uncharted territory, the dark forest of Baba Yaga, the underworld of Pluto and Persephone. Nothing in my mother wanted to go anywhere near this part of her psyche, which was guarded by scorpions. Unaware she may have been, but she knew enough to be frightened. She was forever at odds with the deep and passionate intensity of her own feelings, which, no matter how hard she tried, she could not entirely suppress. Instead, she sloughed them off, let others live them for her, projected them onto those around her, and fought with them there.

Even so, she let me in on a secret; she knew more about suffering—her own and that of others—than she wanted to admit. Still, she held fast to the belief that if she kept her attention on the bright light, darkness would be kept at bay, the sun would never set, and night would never fall. I'm not sure who chose the particularly fierce and violent Psalm that was read at her funeral, but a cousin later remarked that it didn't sound like Aunt Betty at all. He had a point, but I sensed that it accurately expressed the wrath my mother had only been partially aware she carried. I pictured Mozart's Queen of the Night, Lady Macbeth, and any number of witchy women who would step from behind her bright persona and fill a room with the hellish fury of a woman scorned.

But then, "What is the use of having an unhappy anything?," which my mother may or may not have heard Gertrude Stein say that afternoon at the Wednesday Club, sometime after the war.

Seeing the Cézannes

All these years, I have seen Cézanne's paintings in museums in Europe and North America. I have paused and noticed the loveliness characteristic of the French paintings of the period—apples, fabric, figures, light, the sea—and moved on to what I thought of as more interesting work: Modigliani portraits, a gorgeous yellow van Gogh, and the paintings by Chaïm Soutine. My interest was always in the ones who came after Cézanne more than in Cézanne himself.

All these years, I have walked by Cézanne's paintings without really seeing a thing.

Until now.

Something shifted for me, and it had to do with the exhibition *Unscrolled: Reframing Tradition in Chinese Contemporary Art,* in particular the work of Qiu Shihua. I entered a room full of what looked like blank canvases. A sign on the wall suggested standing slightly to the side of each painting and looking at it for a time. I tried that and saw what looked like a warp in the stretcher that buckled the canvas. No. The canvas was flat. I looked and looked—staring and then softening my gaze, and still didn't see much except what looked like water stains or shadows. Then a friend pointed out a path in another smaller painting, and I could see it very faintly, and yet there it was. As I continued to gaze at the canvas, I began to see a landscape emerge, delicate and shadowy, but more and more clearly discernable. These canvases were not about what was on them as much as they were about inviting, indeed forcing viewers to stand in stillness and wait—otherwise nothing would appear. What was there would not be visible until we became still enough to see it.

So I decided to reconsider the Cézannes and tried to see beyond the lovely and lively surface. I began to understand something about the way they were painted, the nature of Cézanne's struggle, and the enormity of his task: to paint reality itself, which is not the same as rendering but is getting at the essence behind and within what we see. The spirit of the thing. Yet not an abstraction.

Cézanne walked the razor's edge between painting as it had been and painting as it was destined to become, at least for a good many years. It was not a question of style, technique, or philosophy. It was a battle waged in the painter's soul when confronting the world he saw—the achingly beautiful and terrible world that lay outside his studio door in Aix-en-Provence.

"The most interesting figure in modern art," D. H. Lawrence writes in 1929, "is Cézanne: and that, not so much because of his achievement as because of his struggle."

Earlier in the essay, Lawrence says, "Our instincts and intuitions are dead, we live wound round with the winding-sheet of abstraction. And the touch of anything solid hurts us. So that Cézanne's apple hurts. It made people shout with pain."

It is Cézanne's ability to make me see and feel the world as reality not abstraction that compelled me to take a deeper look. The longer I stood before his work, the more I came to see Cézanne as a deeply religious painter, not in his subject matter but in his method of working. In one of the letters the poet Rainer Maria Rilke wrote to his wife from Paris in 1907, he says of Cézanne:

With regard to his work habits, he claimed to have lived as a Bohemian until his fortieth year. Only then, through his acquaintance with Pissarro, did he develop a taste for work. But then to such an extent that for the next thirty years he did nothing but work. Actually without joy, it seems, in a constant rage, in conflict with every single one of his paintings, none of which seemed to achieve what he considered to be the most indispensable thing. *La réalisation,* he called it . . .

Heinrich Wiegand Petzet, in his foreword to the collection of Rilke's *Letters on Cézanne,* writes:

> The poet was well aware that he was not only observing a turning point in Western painting . . . But rather, he saw more clearly from day to day that the process revealed in these pictures demanded one's participation, not just one's understanding . . . The poet did not take the teaching he had received as artistic dogma; what had happened, and could happen again to anyone, was the same shock of recognition he had felt before the archaic torso of Apollo: "You must change your life."

Rilke writes: "Surely all art is the result of one's having been in danger, of having gone through an experience all the way to the end, to where no one can go any further."

This insistence on participation and even a sense of the painter having been in danger, underlies the active, lovely surfaces of Cézanne's paintings.

Describing the Cézanne room at the Salon d'Automne, Rilke says: "Here, all of reality is on his side: in this dense quilted blue of his, in his red and his shadowless green and the reddish black of his wine bottles. And the humbleness of all his objects: the apples are all cooking apples and the wine bottles belong in the roundly bulging pockets of an old coat."

Cézanne's attention to the ordinary objects of the world point to his religious feeling, and Rilke often compares Cézanne to van Gogh. Like his Dutch contemporary, Cézanne worked out of deep and consuming love for everything he saw. Not in the least sentimental, this love approached religious awe.

Rilke writes to his wife:

> Today I went to see his pictures again; it's remarkable what an environment they create. Without looking at a particular one, standing in the middle between the two rooms, one feels their presence drawing together into a colossal reality. As if these colors could heal one of indecision once and for all . . . You also notice, a little more clearly

> each time, how necessary it was to go beyond love, too; it's natural, after all, to love each of these things as one makes it: but if one shows this, one makes it less well; one judges it instead of saying it . . . It may be that this emptying out of love in anonymous work, which produces such pure things, was never achieved as completely as in the work of this old man . . .

And in a letter dated four days later: "Behind this devotion, in small ways at first, lies the beginning of holiness: the simple life of a love that endured; that, without ever boasting of it, approaches everything, unaccompanied, inconspicuous, wordless. One's real work, the abundance of tasks, begins, all of it, behind this enduring . . ."

Drawing and Talent

On my way past the Anglican church in my neighborhood, I mentioned to the new rector that I was headed to the studio to do some drawing.

"Oh! How I envy your talent," he said.

I wanted to say: It has nothing to do with talent; it's just making marks. But I didn't want to sound unfriendly.

"Do you ever doodle?" I asked.

"Oh no," he said. "I like to keep things tidy."

Well there's your problem, I thought to myself. That's why you think you can't draw.

"Tidy" is the sworn enemy of nearly everything that interests me.

I couldn't stop thinking about the idea of talent and what it is exactly and whether it can be taught or learned and how we use it to keep ourselves from trying something new. We often talk about developing talent, but what is actually happening? How does talent emerge and evolve in practice? And what does it have to do with what happens when I'm drawing?

Maybe talent describes a proclivity, a desire, a hunger for something. My Anglican friend has an appetite for tidiness. Most likely he is good at keeping things in order; he has a talent for that. I prefer making a mess; that is where my talent lies. Some would call it genius. My mother was always astonished by how not forty minutes after I arrived at her house for a visit, the contents of my suitcase could get themselves distributed—as if strewn—all over the guest room.

When we talk about talent, we often mean aptitude, which calls to mind those awful tests they gave us in school: Would you rather put together a puzzle or visit a sick friend? Ability. Skill. Proclivity.

A literary agent once wrote to me saying that the stories an editor had sent to her showed talent, and she'd like to represent me. I was nearly fifty years old. The work in question was my second collection of short fiction. I wrote back thanking her and said that the real question for me was not talent but whether or not I had anything to say to a contemporary reading public.

Talent suggests a level of competence and these days it is more and more something to be put to use in order to earn a profit. Indeed, the word talent is derived from the medieval Latin talenta, the plural of talentum meaning "inclination, leaning, will, desire"—in classical Latin: "balance, weight; sum of money."

What we have tended to lose sight of is the distinction between a product and the process that was involved in making the product and the value of process for its own sake—the sheer mad pleasure of making something, as well as learning for the sake of knowing, quite apart from its application. We are, once again it seems, in the grip of a weird mix of Puritan utilitarianism and a level of greed that is almost inconceivable. And the real test of talent has become what the final product sells for.

I have drawn all my life. It never occurred to me not to draw. Nobody told me I couldn't. I was even encouraged, given crayons and paper at home, and luckily my early schooling did nothing to discourage me from continuing. In fact my kindergarten and primary-school teachers gave us active encouragement; they knew that we learn by doing. What's more, they believed that our individual experience of the world mattered and called for time and space and attention. They showed a radical trust in the innate curiosity of a child and had the wisdom to know when to get out of the way and when to give guidance. A painful awareness of how rare that privilege is in our school system called me to teaching years later.

At first I drew things that no one but I could identify. I had people around who listened when I described what I'd drawn, and the description usually led into a story about a turtle or frog or my older brother, Charles. I lived in a magical world, and I realized early on that it was my responsibility to remind big people that they lived there too because they kept forgetting. It was tiresome, but as I kept drawing and telling them the stories, they would often add wonderful things to the story that I hadn't thought of, or sometimes a detail that was just wrong, so I told them. They stood corrected. Which didn't last forever of course, but it lasted long enough to give me a solid foundation in the wonder of the world and my ability to participate in its mystery.

Skill, I learned, had to do with drawing in such a way that others recognized that my dog was a dog and the tree was a tree; it meant I had less explaining to do. Drawing was ordinary, a part of the rhythm of my daily life. Sometimes our drawings were put up in the classroom at school or in the hallways. Later they were taken down. They came and went. There were always more where they came from, always a way to make another one. There was nothing precious about them. This is important. They were not yet in any way tied to accomplishment.

That changed in junior high and high school with the ever more intricate selection processes and hierarchies of proficiency—blue, red, and yellow ribbons: first, second, and third place. All of which deadened things somehow. Incompetence saved me in the end. I was never quite good enough at anything to be taken seriously, and so I was left to my own devices, which is exactly what I wanted to be left to as a child.

Even so, at some point, the drawing stopped. Not all at once. It sort of tapered off, but first it went underground—when girls with large pointy breasts started to emerge from the ballpoint pen I now drew with. I had a vague sense that I ought not to be making these drawings. They made me feel funny. I didn't want anybody to see them, and if they had stories associated with them, I didn't want to hear them.

Drawing naturally leads to art, and art leads to art history, and art history leads to—you're a step ahead of me—naked bodies, and the art history book my cousin, two years older than I, had hidden in the boiler room under the Art and Shop Building at our elementary school. Don't ask me how we got in and out, unless no one bothered locking the door, which was probably the case. This is where my secret study of art and the female "form" began. Apparently males didn't have "form," at least not one that interested my cousin. To my unschooled eye, they were all naked bodies, and I was every bit as curious about the one as the other, but there were beginning to be subtle distinctions between curiosities.

My cousin kept our conversations in the boiler room elevated. He would open the book, hold the flashlight, and slowly pronounce the names of painters of the Italian Renaissance. His older brother, Thomas, was already considered to be a gifted painter, though still in high school. His mother was a Christian Scientist, which put their family a few notches above us run-of-the-mill Congregationalists. So I took my cousin seriously; he had pubic hair, which I found fascinating on him but horrifying on me, for any number of reasons I couldn't begin to understand. It was not anything I wanted to draw.

Drawing became more private when I entered seventh grade. Painting was done in a big room together. We all wore smocks over our school clothes, like lab coats that buttoned up the front. In biology, we drew germinating Kentucky Wonder beans in our lab books and then the shoots and leaves as they grew up through the tray of shallow soil. Later on, we were expected to draw the innards of a frog that my lab partner had carefully sliced open with a scalpel. I knew right then and there that biology was not my destiny. At least studying it wasn't. Of course biology had a lot to do with my destiny, but it was happening without my permission and beyond my control. I'm talking here about puberty, of course, and somehow drawing became prurient and secretive.

Drawings are more intimate than paintings, less formal, a way of finding something out about what one is looking at, an inquiry, a rough outline, an impression caught on the fly, just as the light changed or the model turned his head. Marks in a notebook, which one intends to flesh out in more detail later, a quick sketch done on impulse as someone was getting out of the bath. But why women bathing and not men, except maybe when they gathered at the swimming hole? Not inside. Men are not keen on being caught much less observed in such a vulnerable position—buck naked, bent over, drying their toes. No, that would not do. A man had to be in full regalia astride his horse or strategically posed with a crown or miter on his head. Stock-still for his official portrait. A painting, the emblem of his legacy.

Drawings are smaller than paintings; they can be held in the hand. They're less opaque, more open, less filled in. You can see paper through the marks and smudging, a thumbprint, evidence of the human hand at work at closer range than a paintbrush allows. Drawings can be slipped into drawers, pressed between the pages of a book, or tucked carefully into a pocket like a letter. They suggest a quickness, an immediacy, a nimbleness of thought, searching, discovery, changing one's mind, exploring.

It wasn't until I reached college that I took an actual class in drawing. It was agony. The only tool we were allowed to use for the first three weeks was an indelible black marker—to curb the tendency of students to erase everything they put down, said the professor. It was to build our confidence in mark-making, she said. All it did was to fill me with dread. And my drawings were indescribably wonky. I remember trying to draw each brick in the wall of a building and finally giving over to guessing because I was bored stupid. A musician friend and I were the only non–art majors in the course, but he turned out to be a master draftsman, which is to say not only did his drawings actually resemble the thing he was looking at but they had volume and depth, sureness, authority, boldness, and delicacy. I seethed with envy. Mortified doesn't come close to describing what I felt when I pinned my own drawings to the wall for critique. A silence fell upon the studio. I could feel everyone straining to find an encouraging word or two. Even the professor was struck dumb. Especially perplexing were the drawings I did outside class for homework. One seemed to show three reddish brown boulders made of what might have been papier-mâché, which were, in fact, three buckeyes, greatly enlarged, as if seen by a caterpillar. Nonetheless, I stuck with it, finished the course, and, in the words of my professor, I had shown "remarkable improvement."

I have never let my lack of talent stand in the way of something I really wanted to explore. Off I go with a mixture of dogged determination and an airy disregard for competence. The fool in the tarot deck, head pointing one way, feet the other, teetering on the edge of a cliff. Which makes for a more interesting life than trying to prove again and again how much talent you have.

In graduate school at the University of New Hampshire, I audited a night course in figure drawing to take my mind off the early-American sermons and poems I was reading and the piles of student essays I was marking. The drawing professor was a short man who drove up from Boston to teach his classes each week. He wasn't much older than I was, but that did nothing to mitigate the anxiety I felt each time he stopped to watch me as I struggled. I had nearly lost my sense of adventure. Puritan sermons will do that.

"Stand up," he said. "Come back here and look."

I stood beside him.

"What's the difference between the model's shoulder and the shoulder you've drawn?"

"Mine looks dislocated, like she's been in a bad accident."

"Could that shoulder lift anything above its head?"

"No," I said, "I don't believe it could."

"You're drawing it from the outer edge and moving in. Try it the other way round."

He could tell I had no idea what he was talking about.

"You're just looking at the skin. You've forgotten about the musculature and bones underneath. There is a ball-and-socket joint under there as well as twenty different muscles. Once you begin to understand its structure, it'll look more like a shoulder."

I hadn't made much progress by the end of the evening. The professor stopped me on my way out and handed me a book of drawings with a number of pages marked with sticky notes.

"Take this home with you and try copying some of these drawings, noticing how each artist suggests the skeletal structure and muscle, what the artist can't actually see but knows is there."

One of the drawings he had chosen for me was what looked like a quick sketch of a man walking, depicted mid-stride, a study for Rodin's statue of Balzac. A muscular nude with a belly, entirely unselfconscious. A man walking in his own body. Almost exactly where I wasn't. I was living in my head—thinking, rethinking, overthinking everything. Even though I walked a mile and a half to my office and back each day, I was lost in thought, barely aware of my surroundings.

After I ate some supper and prepared for the class I was to teach the following day, I cleared my table, opened the book to Rodin's drawing, and set about to copy it, imitating the gesture that I thought might have resulted in one line or another, holding my charcoal in different ways to achieve various densities of line. Looking. Making marks. A quick one here. A slow one there, making contact with the page, feeling my sit bones on the chair. Extending my own leg to look at my knee and foot. Feeling the stretch and tension as I moved. I was trying to get it "right," but in the process of looking and rendering, something else nosed its way through, a curiosity about the marks themselves, the feel of vine charcoal in my hand, the way Balzac's belly sagged but was also held by the pelvis and propelled by a motion that began at the hip joint, how the weight shifted from back to front leg as he walked, the calf muscles extending as the toes of the back foot prepare to lift, the spaces between the lines. I gasped. I'd been holding my breath. I was aware of the tension in my own neck and shoulder from straining to see. Like it or not, I was in a body that was making itself known to me all day, every day, no matter where my attention was.

A few years ago, I returned to Haystack Mountain School of Crafts, in Deer Isle, Maine, with others who had taught there over the years for some studio time of our own. I installed myself in the drawing studio at a table next to Michael Moore's table. He had recently retired from teaching at the University of Southern Maine and was known for his drawings, some of which he'd done using both hands at once. We gathered our materials and set to work.

Michael sat in front of a large piece of white paper and made marks with chopsticks he had whittled down to various points with a pocketknife. He used black ink—India or Sumi, I forget which—and he just kept making marks on different parts of the paper. After lunch he'd come back to the same drawing and continue. He worked for hours, days, maybe even weeks on a drawing, and yet there was nothing fussy or precious about what he was doing, no sense of a tight compulsion to get it right, but neither was it large and loose. Nothing sloppy about it. There was movement, small areas of concentrated movement, then long (slow, deliberate) lines reaching to another part of the page, where something was moving in an entirely different way. There was a remarkable precision about it.

When I needed a break from my own nervous and restless drawing, I would stand at a reasonable distance from Michael's table and watch him work. A few days in, I asked him how he knew when it was finished.

"When the page is fully activated."

What we're all waiting for, I think, is the moment a drawing shows signs of life, activity, movement. Which is to say the moment a drawing begins to have a life of its own, begins, as it were, to talk back. Which is to say the moment a drawing pulls my glance from one place to another and maybe back again or stops somewhere for no apparent reason. My eye roams, scans back and forth, up and down, and then—and here it gets even more interesting—in. Suddenly I get a feeling of depth. I'm not talking about the learned optical illusion of perspective. No. This is a felt sense of something sinking back and something else stepping forward. A delightful surprise when I notice it.

We tend to think that talent is innate, a God-given gift that bestows effortless ease. To my mind, talent has less to do with DNA than with a willingness, a curiosity, a dogged determination to wait for something to emerge from seemingly random marks, tuning the inner ear to the harmony in the cacophony. Something deeper than mere competence is needed to animate the effort, something more than exercising one's skill. Even if I set out to make a drawing that looks like the person I have in front of me, I need to be willing to enter a call-and-response between the image I see and the marks I am making, a dialogue I've never had before, no matter how many times I've tried to draw the same face.

Talent points to a way of thinking, a decision-making process that runs along the nerves and beneath the level of language, something closer to instinct or dreaming, listening for when the drawing gets too loud or isn't making enough of the right kind of noise, stopping from time to time to take the different and various pulses of a drawing. A way of thinking that naturally gives rise to questions of proportion, balance, the weight of a line, texture, light, shadow, and volume—questions best left for a time when I put down the pencil or charcoal, tape the drawing to the studio wall, and stand back to look. My first questions are: What am I seeing? Where does my eye go? Where does it stop? And what happens next? I cultivate a detached way of observing without opinion, a witness who agrees not to ask formal, analytical questions too early in the process.

More than anything else, drawing demands curiosity, humility, and a willingness to venture into uncharted territory, ready to abandon at each step any preconceived notions. All I can do is be with what is there, right in front of my nose.

Drawing, I would tell my Anglican friend, is less about talent than it is about surrendering to wonder.

The Dear Love of Comrades

I HEAR it is charged against me that I seek to destroy institutions;
But really I am neither for nor against institutions,
. . . .
Only I will establish in the Mannahatta, and in every city of These States, inland and seaboard,
And in the fields and woods, and above every keel little or large, that dents the water,
Without edifices, or rules, or trustees, or any argument,
The institution of the dear love of comrades.

— Walt Whitman

New Hampshire, 1994. I sit in a circle of men. We've been together for three days, telling stories about our fathers, our bodies, our brothers, friends, and lovers; getting naked; learning massage; trusting the safety of the circle; sharing secrets; swapping bad jokes and tall tales; grieving our losses and disappointed dreams. In the course of our time together we have become more and more deeply connected, and I suspect I'm not the only one who doesn't quite believe it. To be this intimate with other men—in community—is somehow unimaginable.

I for one am a loner, not a joiner. However I may long to be included, I am wary of entrapment, loss of liberty, and indoctrination. I need the widest possible lens—and a clear view of all the exits.

In those years, most weekdays at noon, I sat in another circle of men in the basement of the Unitarian Church downtown, where I learned gradually, by close observation, how men carried their pain and stayed sober. Together, we learned how to hold space for the aggression and defensiveness that arose between us and to make room for truth-telling and trust. Together, we learned how to survive our own arrogance, heartbreak, and betrayals. And out of our shared brokenness arose an incomprehensible courage that even the most rugged individualist would be hard-pressed to name as anything but grace.

In those years, I attended a men's retreat during which we considered what it meant to be a warrior. My first thought was it had nothing to do with me; I was a conscientious objector. One man said it was his dad who taught him how to stand up for himself. Another talked about his basketball coach, another a pastor at his church. I heard men talk about what they were willing to fight for and defend, what was important to them, where they drew their line in the sand, how they made their boundaries known. When my turn came, I heard myself say that what I knew about being a warrior I had learned from lesbians. I was surprised because it was true.

And I had never before said it out loud.

Throughout the 1970s in England, France, and the United States, I attended political meetings in which angry young men of the Old Left called for power. Various women would speak up against violence and warn about separating the means from the end. All too often, they were shouted down, derided, and silenced. Then one after another the women rose, gathered their belongings, and headed for the door. Something compelled me to follow them down the street to a pub, a park, or somebody's nearby kitchen table, and for reasons I will never fully understand, they did not ask me to leave. So I sat or stood at the edge of the group and listened. Many but not all of the women were lesbians, and it was in these groups that I received my political education. In these circles, I learned about ethics, integrity, process, dialogue, and consensus. The women called for a far more extensive reevaluation of history than either the male left or the neoliberal establishment were interested in or capable of undertaking. What's more they insisted we explore these questions in ways that engaged more than our intellect, which included the heart, the body, instinct, intuition, and imagination; that acknowledged the more-than-human: animals, forests, rivers; that included ancestors and the world of spirit. We needed every voice and perspective, every organ of perception and facet of consciousness we could access if we were ever to break the cycle of revenge-overthrow-dominance-submission in whose grip we still found ourselves.

I have always encountered my comrades among misfits, outsiders, and nonconformists. American folklore is full of our antics and misadventures, our nimble response to catastrophe and narrow escapes, our alliances with coyote, fox, and raven. Though it may have been born of rejection or exclusion, the role becomes part of our destiny and is not without certain gifts of stealth, swiftness, and cunning. We band together in the margins, form loose connections, tenuous and often temporary, for we are a restless bunch, always on the move, a step ahead of landlords and creditors, not to mention jilted lovers and their spouses. Indeed, my whole generation was born in the restless years after World War II—times of upheaval, uprooting, revolution, and seemingly aimless wandering.

I spent a great deal of time alone in my first four years. My siblings were all quite a bit older, and there were no children my age in the neighborhood. I learned to keep my own company and found ways to amuse myself while those around me were busy with other things. Once I started school, I felt a little behind as far as socialization was concerned. Other kids seemed to understand things about games and running in herds, which I found perplexing. They appeared to have mastered the push-pull give-and-take laws of the sandbox, and I had a time of it catching up. Teachers often commented on my tendency to withdraw—and observe. I was, in fact, watching very carefully.

A few years ago, I reconnected with Chris, one of my first friends from elementary school. We'd lost touch when his family moved away from St. Louis after seventh grade. We were both going to be in Portland, Oregon, and decided to meet. Once our eyes adjusted to each other's white hair, weight gain, and crow's-feet, we were able to pick up where we'd left off fifty-five years earlier. In one of those weird ticks in the time-space continuum, the boys we had been back then were there with us, remembering themselves and each other in these two older men sitting over breakfast in a hotel dining room. As we reminisced, we realized that both of our families had been in crisis in those years. His mother was in and out of psychiatric wards, and the tension in my house around my father's drinking had neared the breaking point. It's as if we had known without knowing, certainly without speaking, sensing in the way friends sense, by instinct, how to support each other through hardships we never spoke of directly because they were secret and shameful. That morning as we sat over coffee, I realized that my survival and whatever sanity I managed to hang on to through those years depended, in part, upon the love and companionship of friends like Chris.

Then came puberty—trial by fire. A wild heat pulled my attention to the nether regions of my body—down there. Shocked, surprised, confused, excited, repulsed, and terrified, I became by turns giddy and tearful. And no amount of biological information or the wise counsel of the school psychologist or the basketball coach succeeded in relieving my distress. As for my parents, forget it—they were worse than useless. A deep chasm opened and I was never quite sure if I was falling in or climbing out. The secret life I had held so lightly as a child suddenly became dangerous. I grew ever more evasive, moody, and belligerent. I took a vow of silence and skulked around with a long face.

My friendships became more complex and trickier to navigate. I studied who was in and who was out and why. I tried on various personae. I was, in fact, trustworthy and became known as a good egg, harmless, a class clown, not a contender in the middle- and high-school pecking order. I allied myself with kids who would provide protection against predators. And as for the bullies, I held the power of secrets shared in confidence with their girlfriends and teammates. Go-between and mediator, I remained autonomous, an independent agent. I learned about deeper loyalties and betrayal. I learned whom I could trust with my own secrets, who had information about sex that was actually useful, and who knew what was happening in the world outside our white suburban bubble.

Spenser was a big friendly guy who joined our seventh-grade class, and everyone liked him immediately. He lived in a town on the Missouri River, a forty-minute drive from the school, so he was an outsider, and I offered him an in because I'd gone to elementary school with a number of the kids who were shaping up to be the cool group. We took to each other right away and earned each other's trust quickly, which I suspect had something—a lot—to do with my sister Carol, who was a senior that year. She was generally and genuinely loved by students and teachers alike for her stamina, good humor, and the dignity with which she carried her pain since becoming ill with Crohn's disease. She remained mischievous, fun-loving, and a loyal friend. Spenser's sister had also faced serious medical crises. The three of us were kindred in some way, and Carol right away recognized Spenser's maturity and good sense. She was worried about leaving me alone with our parents, who were at each other's throats more and more. So she deputized Spenser in a manner of speaking and entrusted me to his wisdom. Spenser was just the right mix of adventure and prudence. Our friendship was heartfelt, open, and honest. He was someone I could trust and lean into. At thirteen, he was already a mensch, a friend, a role model, coconspirator, and brother. He and friends like him got me through high school more or less intact.

Once released into the wide world, I started to unravel. I entered college with both a sense of liberation and a deep anxiety about the world, the war, my draft status, my sexuality, my intellectual capability, and my sanity. I started college in Wisconsin, wandered around Europe, lived for a time in England, returned to St. Louis, hit a kind of bottom, resurfaced, graduated from college, moved to France, then Spain, then back to England before returning to the States—chaotic years marked by a sense of fear that defies description or clear diagnosis. The more ground I covered, the smaller my world became.

And yet, despite betrayals, evasions, heartbreak, and alcoholic blackouts, somehow, thanks to the dogged grace of friendship, people managed to get through to me from time to time and, due to my own persistence working from within, I was sometimes able to encounter what I was too proud and scared to admit I longed for.

My travels became less frenetic. I landed in stages; the distances between places grew smaller—from northern Vermont to southern New Hampshire to Portland, Maine, where I settled for the next twenty-six years. I met people through work, fellow part-time faculty at the university, and various other jobs I had—cigar-shop clerk, bookseller, house cleaner, group-home supervisor, tour guide at Henry Wadsworth Longfellow's boyhood home. I settled into various overlapping circles of friends, people I came to count on and lean into for support, and though many of us had come from away, over time, we were woven into the fabric of life in Maine.

We gathered for weddings, funerals, feast days, and each time we came together, whether in crisis or in celebration, we extended, deepened, and amplified our friendship and kinship ties, the very substance of community. And because of who we were and the way Maine is, we remained just outside the American mainstream, resistant to the manic surge of the 1980s, which tipped into the national paranoia of the early 2000s. To be sure, we were not immune, but the contagion seemed to be slowed by our ethos of common sense, letting people be, lending a hand when someone needed help, no matter who they may have voted for in the last election.

What, then, is the spark that ignites friendship in the first place? What draws us out of the cave of solitude? Pheromones? A glance? A tone of voice? I wonder who you are, what's possible between us, who I might become, what kind of mischief, mirth, or grace we might get up to. What wild hope or spirit of adventure urges us on? We step forward, withdraw, advance again, boldly, then tenderly probe the space between us. Will it nourish, affirm, sustain life? How much of us can it hold? What are we being called to create, protect, or heal?

Something in the world we have created for ourselves seems to want to prevent our coming together, turning to one another, talking about our lives as they are and not as we want them to appear. Something in this world of ours seems to depend upon our being at odds, competitive, even predatory, focused on our frenzied consumption of goods and resources. For if we listened with our whole being, fully embodied, and addressed the heart of the matter, we might loosen the grip of whatever compulsion, delusion, or fantasy has us in its thrall.

Some years back, I heard people talk about how a colonial power ends up colonizing itself using the same means by which it colonized others—disappearing the elders, destroying the rituals, defiling the sacred places—effectively erasing its own memory. Kinship ties and communities dissolve, leaving only alienation and despair. Which more and more describes the world we find ourselves in today.

Yet something survives. Fungi, mosses, ferns, shoots, buds. Nothing we have invented can entirely wipe out the memory of rebirth, the biological imperative. And so it is with wonder, kinship, love. Papyrus fragments found in mummy wrappings. Charred pages of a partially burned book. Syllables of a nearly forgotten language still spoken by one old woman who lives at the edge of the wood. With one thread and then another, we begin to reweave the sacred story. The thing once forced underground resurfaces and spreads. Again and again curiosity and desire rouse us from sleep, and as if pulled by some magnetic force, we find ourselves walking alongside a stranger, wondering what's on their mind, where they're headed and why, what they're about, and whether or not they want company. We listen, we prod, we ponder, we enthuse, commiserate, empathize. We seek confluence; we meet divergence. We joke. We complain. We go on walking for the simple pleasure of spontaneous movement, the shared joy of being alive in a body, never straying far from the animal energy, which is what brought us together in the first place. Once again friendship shows its persistence in reawakening and setting forth, following its own powerful impulse to explore the terrain, seek out life, create. And we are reminded, again and again, that against the dear love of comrades, tyranny doesn't stand a chance.

An Interview with Lynda Barry

American cartoonist Lynda Barry—best known for her comic strip, *Ernie Pook's Comeek*—is also a novelist, philosopher, and champion of an unpopular cause: calling attention to the unintended impact of industrial-scale wind turbines on a rural community. Her book *Picture This: The Near-sighted Monkey Book* explores where drawing happens, why it doesn't, and all that drawing can be.

"I wanted to figure out a way to write about drawing that didn't involve writing about drawing," she says. "I wanted to make some stuff on the page that as soon as you saw it, it made you want to make stuff on a page."

Take her Recipe for Depression, for example: "gluing wads of sadness on a chicken."

"Drawing isn't the thing that's left on paper," she says. "That's not where it happens. It's an experience."

For Barry, drawing is a process that begins well before we put pencil to paper.

"When you were a kid on a long car ride," she continues, "there's lots of staring—at stains on the back of the front seat, for example—and if you stare at them, they turn into stuff. That counts as drawing. You don't have to physically make a picture. You're taking this thing and relaxing until an image presents itself to you—clouds, let's say—that counts as drawing."

Once we've begun to make marks, drawing has everything to do with hands and motion.

"A completely different kind of story is available when you write by hand," she says. "Also graphically. Something different happens. The happy accident gets undone on Photoshop. When you don't see immediate value, you delete it. Let's say I want to draw, and I start drawing. I'm liking it, and then I do something that starts to kill the drawing. It's dying! Give it CPR! The thing you're doing to keep it from dying is the real drawing."

Picture This was completely handmade. Barry pasted all of the images onto pages with Elmer's school glue.

"We didn't have money growing up. We never had art supplies. We used whatever was right there—Q-tips and watercolors, ball-point pen, pencil, glue, scissors, a ruler. That's it."

What was important was the act of playing.

"We have a tacit understanding of the connection between mental health and playing. The one thing almost everyone knows around the world is that a kid who's never allowed to play is crazy by twenty-one. I'm really interested in the brain and what's going on. Now they can put a shower cap with a million wires on the head of toddler and an artist and look at what the brain is doing in creative concentration in the adult and deep play in the child. Their brains look identical in that the whole brain is activated. This thing called 'the arts' is something we've been doing forever—as important as opposable thumbs. When you are shamed out of the thing that helps you stay not crazy . . . we're in trouble."

Luckily, Barry often works in schools, with students and teachers alike.

"I'm trying to figure out a way to teach painting without interfering. I start painting and if somebody wants to paint, I dip their brush in and say, 'Make a mark.' I watch them. They get gorgeous lines, and I've seen some weird ways of holding the brush."

She was once asked to present a workshop at a design conference.

"Hotshot designers!" She laughs. "Those guys didn't want to touch the brush; they were freaked out by it. I had to invent a game. I said, 'Divide the page in half and in half again until you can't divide it anymore. But if the lines touch, you get electrocuted.' It changed from making a drawing to play."

People fill her workshops, saying they wish they could draw.

"Look," says Barry, "if you're stuck on the phone, you doodle. Eyeballs, whatever. Okay. That's all that's left for a lot of people but that's all it takes. It's weird for adults—unless we know why or what it's for, we won't do it. When I sit down with six-year-olds, they don't ask 'What's our budget?'"

When Barry isn't thinking about drawing, writing, and creativity, she finds herself active in making people aware of the impact of huge wind turbines being used to generate electricity in rural Wisconsin. A nearby national wildlife refuge is being affected by eighty-five industrial-scale wind turbines (each one is forty stories tall) that are two miles away. The bat population is threatened, for one. Wisconsin now has the second-highest bat kill rate in the United States. And energy developers are lobbying to build more turbines within one mile of the refuge. Other turbines have been built closer to people's houses and farms. And this has caused real problems for many of her neighbors. In principle, Barry supports alternative energy sources. She and her husband heat with wood. They cook with wood. They have no clothes dryer.

"We were all about the wind," she says. "But the way the developers were talking, I got this sick feeling. They were so slick."

So Barry started doing research. At a public hearing in the state capital, people complained that they couldn't sleep because of the noise of the turbines. They asked legislators to come stay in their homes, so they could see for themselves. Barry volunteered.

"I didn't say I was a cartoonist. They call for an ambulance, and I show up in a clown car!"

When she visited them, she began to see there was a problem. So she decided to follow twenty families, interviewing them and making videos. People's health was deteriorating due to lack of sustained sleep. Normally fit people were getting fat due to a low-frequency thump that affected the organs and the body's ability to process glucose. One family finally abandoned their home out of desperation.

"What makes me crazy," says Barry, "is no one's listening. I saw these wind developers using legislation to bully local communities. I don't like bullies. I never have."

And here the story takes an interesting turn. Many of her neighbors are at the other end of the political spectrum from Barry.

"I'm a liberal with a capital L," she explains, "and many of them are evangelical Christians. One of my neighbors invited me to church. My stomach turned. I girded my loins to sit through—whatever. And they never mentioned liberals once. I was disappointed. It was like a regular church service. It didn't occur to me that they would do anything else but demonize liberals. When the other side becomes human to you—being with these families and seeing how much misery they're in—it's difficult to be smug. Polarization opens the door for corporate greed. If neighbors aren't communicating, it allows for something very bad to come in. It's done wonders for me knowing conservatives. It's been life-transforming."

Teaching/Writing

I couldn't have cared less about teaching writing. I needed a place to live. I had just moved back to the States, having failed to make a life for myself in England. I needed time to get my bearings, and graduate school would give me a couple of years to read American literature, to find out what made it American and not just a derivative of British literature. The University of Vermont offered me a teaching assistantship, which meant I was to earn my keep by teaching English composition, not exactly everybody's favorite course. I was invited to attend a conference on the teaching of writing that summer on campus, so I went. As I said, to find a place to live.

I arrived a day early, so I could begin my search for housing, but also to meet with the chair of the English Department to talk about how I might best shape my course of study over the next two years. I sat down full of enthusiasm with questions about the nature of the American mind and how it had evolved through literature. Behind a highly polished mahogany desk sat a stern, slender, stiff-necked man, the very image of Ichabod Crane.

"Mr. DePew," he said, and I knew I was already in some kind of trouble. "You have these gaps. Chaucer," he said. "And the Victorians—to name but a few."

"But I came here to study American literature," I said.

"That may well be," he said, "but in order to pass our comprehensive examination, you'll need to do something about these gaps."

"Couldn't I take a comprehensive exam in American lit?"

"Are you suggesting we write a special exam just for you?"

"Well, why not?"

There I sat at the first of many impasses I was to encounter in northern New England over the next thirty years.

Added to this irritation was what the other conference participants were saying about Donald Murray, the teaching writing guru from the University of New Hampshire. Don Murray says this. Don Murray says that. He had more quotations than Chairman Mao. I wasn't interested. And I couldn't have been in a fouler mood as I walked into Murray's first session the next morning.

Don was a great bear of a man, upbeat and affable, with a deep booming voice. I hated him on sight. He started by putting his work in context. He based his teaching model on what he knew as a journalist about how professional writers practiced their craft. Writing is a process, he explained, and yet as teachers all we look at is the finished product, which, more often than not, isn't finished because we haven't given the student enough time. He proposed that we slow down, open up the process, paying attention to how writing actually happens instead of just assessing the outcome. No one, he said, taught writing in this way aside from the University of New Hampshire, a handful of schools in Vermont, and a few places in California.

Oh really, I thought. No one? I sat in the back row with my arms crossed. I may have even rolled my eyes.

"Not even in St. Louis, Alfred," said Murray.

I sat up straight. That he knew my name didn't throw me, but how did he know I was from St. Louis? And how did he know what I was thinking? Most unsettling of all, he had found a chink in my armor and seen straight through it to the writer in me who had been silenced.

He led us through an exercise using index cards. On the first one, he had us list twenty-five details about a person, place, or thing. On the next one, we wrote a paragraph using a few of the most vivid details on our list. On the third card, he asked us to rewrite the paragraph, incorporating any changes we might want to make. When we finished, he asked if anyone wanted to read their paragraph and talk about the choices they had made. The room came alive. Everyone wanted to continue writing.

"Well all right, then," said Murray. "We have some time before and after lunch. See how far you can get into a first draft and bring it to this afternoon's session. See you at two o'clock."

The next day we each had a conference with the Great Man himself. He had me read what I'd brought in and then asked me what I heard going on in the draft.

"I don't know," I said. "It seems all over the place. I'm not even sure what it's about. There's so much more to this story."

"There usually is," he said, grinning, and we both laughed.

After telling me which parts caught and held his attention, he suggested I think about what I was working on as a section of what might become a longer essay.

He had listened, really listened. He was honest-to-god curious about what was happening in this piece of writing—and what would happen next. What's more, he seemed to have every confidence that I would find my way simply because he knew this process from the inside out. Every morning without fail, he sat at his desk at home and wrote for a few hours before he left for the university to teach.

Something happened to me in that three-day seminar that's hard to describe. I felt actual space opening up around me as I wrote. I had room to change my mind. I could hear myself think, not just in the usual worried loops but in a flow that carried me into deeper, fuller currents of thought. I'd come to Burlington, Vermont, to find a place to live, which I did—a room in a boardinghouse on Maple Street. But I also found the place where I felt most alive: talking to writers about writing.

I remember nothing about the first classes I taught in the fall. I was terrified and overwhelmed. In those days, graduate fellows in the English Department had full responsibility for two sections of composition, which the registrar tried to keep to twenty students per class. We were expected to meet with each student individually once a week to discuss their essays in progress in addition to the regularly scheduled three hours of class. This on top of the coursework in our own two graduate seminars. English composition was a hybrid of process and content, skills and experience. Students were expected to reach some level of competence in the rhetorical modes—narration, description, comparison/contrast, argument—as well as write a research paper. The graduate students met regularly with the other faculty members teaching the course to address questions and concerns. My student conferences felt natural to me, but I struggled with leading class discussion and keeping up with the syllabus. It was the intimacy, the attentive listening in individual conferences that really moved students forward.

One young man came in to discuss his research topic: the legalization of marijuana.

"What most interests you about the topic?" I asked.

"Nothing," he said. "I don't even smoke the stuff."

"Then why write about it?"

"It's controversial. Aren't research papers supposed to be about controversial issues?"

"Sometimes. Not always. Even so, isn't there something that interests you more than marijuana?"

"Sure," he said, "basketball."

"What interests you about basketball?"

"I don't know. I like to play. That's all."

"Who's your favorite team?"

"The New York Knicks."

"How are they doing?"

"Terrible. They suck!"

"Why do you suppose that is?"

"Everyone wants to be a superstar. No real teamwork."

Maybe that's your subject. Something about basketball."

He sat for a moment, thinking, then said, "You know what really gets me? The way sports scholarship students are treated. Recruiters offer all kinds of money, cars, even prostitutes to sign them, and once they're in school, they don't have a life. They can't even study what they came to college to study."

"Sounds like you're onto something. Bring in a draft and a list of possible reference articles, and we'll see where it's going."

Then there was the young woman who didn't show up for her conferences, and when she turned in work, it was half-baked, no real energy or interest, not just begrudging but downright hostile. When she did come for a conference I asked her what was going on. And she leveled with me. She wanted to study journalism, but her dad insisted she study engineering.

"Well then," I said. "Write about that."

"I already have," she said and pulled a sheaf of papers from her backpack.

As she read it to me, I began to hear from the person who had been hiding behind the resentment, and she had a strong, clear, confident, voice. The writing was resonant, insightful, vivid, and alive. We sat for a moment when she'd finished.

"Here's the good news," I said. "That's one of the strongest pieces of writing I've had from anyone all semester."

"And the bad news?"

"Now that I know what you're capable of, I expect nothing less than your best effort from here on in."

She looked relieved and started gathering her belongings.

"The other good news," I said, "is that nothing says you have to stop writing once you're an engineer. Biologists, piano tuners, nurses, auto mechanics, all kinds of people write great essays all the time. One of America's finest poets sold insurance for a living. Another one delivered babies. Something to think about."

Then there was the problem of grading. At the beginning of the fall term we gathered for a workshop on evaluating student work. Our faculty supervisor handed out two anonymous essays for us to read, grade, and explain why we'd given it the grade we had. Then we discussed our decisions as a group. Essay #1 was about a student's pet rock, a fad among American teenagers, which I hadn't heard about. The essay rambled a bit and had its share of grammatical errors and spelling mistakes, but it made me laugh out loud. I gave it a B-. It was clearly above average in its imagination and strong voice, its vivid detail, humor, and sheer aliveness and engagement. Everyone else gave it a D. It was disorganized, they said. It had no real point. It was not, someone said, college-level work. Essay #2 outlined the advantages of a liberal arts education. It was well organized, well argued, with no serious grammar infractions or misspellings. "This," pronounced one of my colleagues, "is as good as student writing gets."

"Oh please!" I cried. "It's dead, voiceless, unoriginal, and most likely a repeat performance." It sounded like any number of essays students regularly submitted as part of their college applications. I remembered writing something similar myself. I gave it a C+/B-. It was solid college-level writing, for sure, but nothing remarkable. I wanted to see the students challenge themselves, take more risks. Everyone else gave it an A. The debate that followed got quite heated. How much weight should be given to originality if the piece was incoherent? We weren't teaching creative writing; we were teaching exposition. Fair enough, I said, but the writer fails to convince me that they believe what they're saying—much less care. That's entirely subjective, said another person. Our job is to teach logic, clarity, and development of thought to ensure that our students are successful in their college careers. But what do we really mean by college-level writing or standard English usage? I said. And who decides that? Isn't it shaped by class and race? These were not questions that particular group was willing to address in 1978, questions we tackled fearlessly and from many points of view once I got to the University of New Hampshire.

It became clear in the following months that I was pretty thoroughly misaligned with the English faculty at UVM and its graduate program, so I moved on to the University of New Hampshire to continue my studies and found a community more compatible with my interests as a scholar and my philosophy as an educator. Murray was our teaching supervisor. Many in the School of Education were studying the writing process in children and adolescents. And those who taught American literature were wholehearted in their enthusiasm and rigor. The place was alive with excitement.

But the problem of grading student work persisted. How could grading serve learning and not stop it dead in its tracks? How to weave evaluation into the writing process and make it something other than a system of punishment or reward? There I was, doing everything I could to ensure that the writer maintained the authority of their experience and writing. Then I turn around to assert the final authority of the almighty grade. Which in fact was part of my job. What a terrible betrayal, especially in the case of students who made steady progress, showed improvement, and learned a great deal but whose work at the end of the term was still not up to snuff. But what was this "snuff" we were all supposed to be up to? A question that became especially vexing a few years later when I started teaching in a remedial writing program at the University of Southern Maine, whose students had fallen through almost every conceivable crack in the education and social welfare systems.

I wanted students to learn to evaluate their own work, which meant learning to read a piece of writing in progress—a very different way of reading. Normally when we pick up a magazine or book, we read for information; it's interesting or boring, useful or not, we like it or we don't. Reading a working draft, a piece of writing that is finding its way to completion, requires a soft focus, an open mind, and curiosity of a different order. Asking the wrong question of a piece of writing in process can mean certain death. Some writers never survive and stop writing altogether.

In the course of schooling, we learn to read critically. It's a useful way to read: assessing, evaluating, questioning are all essential to critical thinking, inquiry, and intellectual discourse. But they can be fatal when reading a work in progress, especially our own. One must develop a willing suspension of critical judgment and a heightened curiosity about what is emerging in the draft in all of its various potentialities. At this stage, our inner editor has no place and must be kept out of the room altogether, with the assurance that they will be invited back when needed—toward the end of the process. Editors can be touchy, easily offended, so it's not about discounting their function, which is essential. It's about knowing when to engage it.

In a conference with a writer, evaluation begins with questions like: What is this draft shaping up to be about? Where do you think it is going? What changes do you want to make in the next draft? In workshops, writers turn their attention to the work in progress of their fellow writers. I developed simple guidelines about what we were listening for and how to respond in a way that would be helpful to the writers in revising their work. We focused on two questions: What did you find strongest about this draft? What questions do you have for the writer? Period.

Once the writer had read the draft out loud, I had them sit outside the circle and take notes as we shared the draft's strengths and the questions that came up for us. This made it easier for writers to hear what their readers were getting from the actual draft—without interjecting disclaimers or apologies or explanations. It's essential for writers to hear what is speaking most clearly to their readers and to discern which of the readers' questions will or will not be useful to them in writing the next draft. Then the writer rejoins the circle to tell us what they learned and to ask any clarifying questions. The writer remains in charge of the piece of writing.

Toward the end of a semester I had students choose what they felt to be their three most successful essays for a final edit, as if they were submitting them for publication. I met with each student to discuss their choices and their reasons for selecting the essays they had chosen. In other words, what were their criteria for good writing? Accompanying their final drafts, I asked them to include a paragraph or two about why the essays they'd chosen represented their best work as well as what they had learned in the process. I also had them give each essay a grade and give themselves an overall grade for the course.

Once again, my job was to honor their choices and not to override their decisions. This was not as easy as I make it sound. However much I stood behind my philosophical principles, I worried about a number of things—my own authority as "professor" when I was in fact untenured, part-time casual labor; what did and did not qualify as "college-level writing"; grade inflation; and the swift and steady decline in American literacy.

Never mind insecurities about my own writing.

Early on in my teaching, I realized I was not doing what I asked my students to do in their writing—experiment, try things out, and head into difficult topics because they mattered. I was up against an old fear, which I saw my students overcoming in themselves again and again. I considered bringing my own essays into the workshop for feedback, but it seemed inappropriate, somehow, and in any event, I lost my nerve.

My writing had become more and more circumspect in high school, and whatever fear I had developed swallowed me whole once I got to college. A combination of adolescent self-consciousness and a monstrous inferiority complex kept me from the easy confidence—even bravado—I saw in other undergraduates. Then there were the terrifying stories I heard about what went on in creative writing seminars on campus. It was the age of encounter groups and the psychological striptease of confessional poets. All of which froze my mind, so I stuck to learning the fundamentals of literary criticism and read everything I could get my hands on: Anaïs Nin, Lawrence Durrell, Virginia Woolf, Henry Miller to name a few. I wrote expository essays for class and recorded everything else in a secret notebook—a litany of insecurities and a merciless self-criticism that would have been envy of any Chinese student during the Cultural Revolution.

The writing that beckoned to me from the edges of my scholarly work in graduate school kept pointing to the body. The fiction and poetry I was studying, student essays I was reading, indeed life itself pulled me into scenes in physical locations with people interacting as a way of illustrating ideas. I wondered how a particular theory or aspect of literary history lived in my body. The portal, more often than not, was emotion. What was it like for the eighteenth-century Quaker John Woolman to travel from one Friends meeting to another, expressing his objections to slavery, and waiting with his fellow Friends for the guidance of the Spirit? And how different it must have felt to be Benjamin Lay, another early-American Quaker who was far more strident in his objections to slavery. I pondered how the enslaved Eliza and her husband, George Harris, in Harriet Beecher Stowe's *Uncle Tom's Cabin,* needed to be able to imagine what freedom might be like, had to feel it in their bones, before they undertook the arduous journey north to Canada, the only place where real freedom was possible for them after the passage of the Fugitive Slave Act of 1850.

Once I moved to Maine, I tried my hand at fiction. I wrote a few short stories, one of which I used to apply to a summer writing conference at the university. I was accepted, and the story was covered in the first workshop. When we met individually, the instructor tried to give helpful suggestions to improve the story, but it felt finished to me. It had done its job, gotten me into the conference, and I was at work on other stories. To put it another way, the instructor and I sat outside and not inside the story, which is where you need to sit with a writer when a story is emerging.

Each evening the writing instructors would read from their own work. The novelist Carolyn Chute was there that year, riding the wave of success of her first novel, *The Beans of Egypt Maine.* I was struck as much by her lack of pretense as I was by the vivid pictures she created in my mind as she read. When I met with her the next morning, I brought a piece I was still working on, so we were able to enter it together and wonder out loud about it. I appreciated her generosity, her wisdom, and her enormous heart, which was not the least bit sentimental.

That evening, Dianne Benedict read a story from her collection, *Shiny Objects,* in a voice that was so soft it was barely audible from my seat in the back row. I closed my eyes, straining to hear, my mind filling with images as the story unfolded—vivid, yet mysterious. Ethereal somehow. I felt the presence of the unseen and unknowable in and among the objects of daily life. A mutual friend had written, urging me to study with her, so I approached Dianne afterward to thank her and ask if I might audit one of her evening seminars in the fall. Why yes, she said. By all means.

And so my apprenticeship in the practice of fiction began. Dianne's way of talking about writing and her way of teaching were deeply resonant with my own. She had been influenced by the pedagogy of the Austrian mystic Rudolf Steiner, whose work I had encountered indirectly, through people who had attended Waldorf Schools. Listening lay at the heart of it all—listening not just to the words themselves but also to what one sensed was moving underneath. "Pay attention to what you may think is a cliché," she said.

"There's usually a genuine feeling inside once you break it open." Gradually, I learned to apply what I knew as a teacher to my own writing, which meant I had to read my manuscripts in progress with the same broad attention and detached curiosity I gave to my students' drafts.

The practice of fiction freed me from any number of habitual snags and constraints. Write about what you know was the famous injunction. But all I seemed to know was my own story, which always came down to the same list of misdeeds, shortcomings, excuses, regrets, and resentments. When I stepped into what Dianne called the "wholly imagined," I found myself in a broad, open plain with an enormous sky, free to engage with whoever came striding toward me. I imagined my way into minds and lives not my own, and in so doing, I discovered surprising empathy and insights. My own story interested me far less than the stories I found that I carried within.

After a few years, Dianne suggested I begin thinking of the stories I was writing as a collection. But they were all so different, I said. I thought a collection had to have a distinctive voice, a comprehensive vision, or a style. I didn't see any unifying themes. You won't, said Dianne, until you begin putting them together. And so I did. I included one of the stories in my application for a Maine Arts Commission Fellowship and was awarded one. Surprised and emboldened, I entered the whole collection in two competitions: the Iowa Short Fiction Award and the Flannery O'Connor Award, and I won the latter.

Which both delighted and frightened me. Months later, while proofreading the final galleys, I didn't like the idea that strangers would be able to read the book without my permission. I wanted to call the whole thing off. Even though the characters in my stories were not me, at least in any autobiographical sense, in another sense they were expressions of me in the way that every figure in a dream is an aspect of the dreamer. Or as Milan Kundera suggests in *The Unbearable Lightness of Being,* our fictional characters are our "own unrealized possibilities." I felt exposed.

Don't get me wrong. There's a lot I enjoyed about publishing my first book. Newspaper and radio interviewers revealed what was in the stories—themes, threads, questions, points of connection. And there is nothing more satisfying than seeing one's book in the window of a local bookstore. I was a part of my community in a whole new way.

But there were drawbacks as well. When I settled down to write again, I banged out a few paragraphs on my typewriter, but they weren't quite right. I started over. I kept stopping. That was the first distress signal: I worried about the outcome before I had even started. For I now knew what I was doing. I had won a fellowship and a literary prize. I had proved myself. And I was paralyzed. I dared not make one false move, for fear that the finished story might be rejected by *The New Yorker,* might disappoint my inflated expectations, which had begun to include a real teaching job at a real university—full time with benefits, a modest bungalow near campus, tweed jackets with leather patches at the elbows, lunches with my editor in the city, which didn't have to be New York, it could be Boston, or Chicago, or Minneapolis. I might even start smoking a pipe.

I was in deep trouble. I couldn't write a word. There was not one shred of joy, no real curiosity or wonder in what I was doing. I had become competent. Intuition nudged me to sign up for an evening painting class at the art school in the fall, and Painting for the True-Blue Beginner turned out to be exactly what I needed. Every Thursday night, I stood dumbfounded and clueless, squeezing mounds of oil paint onto palette paper, adding too much or too little linseed oil, trying to match the colors of the fruit in the bowl on the table around which we had gathered our easels. Oh what a mess I made. I was having the time of my life! At the end of the evening, my canvas was filled with gollywhompus bananas and apples in a misshapen bowl. In the intervening days, I could hardly wait to get back into the studio on Thursday night. Everything that had drained out of my writing life—inquiry, discovery, a sense of play, in other words: freedom—was slowly being restored to me as I failed again and again to make paint do what I wanted it to do. For it had a mind of its own, paint did, and I had to surrender.

Once again, the challenge was to bring what I was learning in the painting studio to my time at the typewriter. I had something in mind to write; it felt longer than a story. Though I loved reading novels, I knew nothing about writing one. I knew enough to sense that it was more than just a long story. A novel had more movable parts, demanded a different quality of mind and much more room to move around in. All I knew was that I didn't know what I was doing, which lightened my heart and made me giddy with exhilaration at the prospect of stepping into unfamiliar territory.

And northern New Mexico provided me with the perfect place.

I had applied for and received a three-month fellowship at an artist colony in Taos, which meant I could work on this mysterious new longer piece of fiction free of the distractions and demands of my daily life in Maine. The drive across the country, the change in scenery along the way, and the strangeness of the high desert all served to lift me out of my doldrums and set me in motion again.

Along about this time, I was feeling the need to shift something in my teaching at the art school. I had fallen into a joyless grind through the syllabus, a survey of world literature, which loosely paralleled the students' art history timeline. Somehow I had lost the dynamism of the writing workshops I offered through the art school's continuing studies program and the Maine Writers and Publishers Alliance. Inspired by the writing practices taught by Natalie Goldberg, Julia Cameron, Linda Trichter Metcalf, and Tobin Simon, I took to beginning each class with ten minutes of free writing. Anyone who wanted to read what they'd written could do so, but no one was obliged. No comments or feedback. We just listened. Then we headed into our discussion of *Gilgamesh* or *Antigone* or whatever text we were studying together.

It wasn't long before we established our rhythm. We entered the classroom, sat down, and got out our notebooks. I'd set the timer for ten minutes, and we'd write until the bell sounded and we stopped. Students were shy about reading at first, but it didn't take long before more and more of them decided to read, having been affected by hearing others. Though we made no comments, when we heard something funny, naturally we laughed; when something moved us, it showed in our faces and seemed to change something in the air. Again and again, students were surprised by the power of their own voices and the experience of being heard in a way they may not have been heard before. I also read when I felt moved to, and over time we got to know each other in ways we wouldn't have ordinarily. Each group began to experience itself more as a community and not just another roomful of art students suffering through Plato's *Symposium* or *Sir Gawain and the Green Knight.* The writing practice seemed to shift even those discussions. Different kinds of questions arose as we deepened and broadened our own experience of writing. Some said this new sense of connection overflowed into their studio classes and critiques—something I had been trying to accomplish for a good number of years.

As part of the Maine Art Commission's Touring Artists program, I sometimes received invitations to visit schools around the state to work with student writers. Whenever I could, I accepted, with one condition—that I also offer a workshop for teachers. Most schools were delighted to get this added value at no extra charge. My hands-down most successful of these residencies was on Mount Desert Island, where the middle and high school managed to engage every student, regardless of temperament or skill level. MDI had more energy and spirit than I had encountered in most other schools. Students were willing to take risks, were generous in the attention they gave to one another, and for some reason hadn't formed rigid cliques. Excited to have their own workshop, the teachers asked if I'd be willing to offer one in the evenings for parents and anyone else in town who might be interested.

You bet, I said. So that very evening, we sat in the Grange Hall in a loose circle, notebooks on our knees.

"Okay," I said. "Let's write for ten minutes about winter boots."

"What about winter boots?" asked somebody.

"Anything you know, remember, or think about them. Just follow your thought, see where it goes. It's an experiment. It's about—well let's find out what it's about."

Who in Maine doesn't have something to say about winter boots? We heard stories about leaky boots, one lost boot, ski boots, galoshes, and the legendary Canadian Sorel. We listened with astonishment, empathy, and great good humor. One memory seemed to spark another. I threw out another prompt and then another. We wrote. We read. Then I asked for ideas from the circle. "First kiss!" someone called out. Everybody laughed. A few teenagers turned scarlet. And we were off for another ten minutes. At the end of the evening, we looked around at one another. No one had expected we'd have this much fun, or remember so many stories, or feel so moved. We were all changed, however slightly, and maybe they would see each other or treat each other a little differently in the coming days. I had no way of knowing. But in that moment, at least, the world seemed a friendlier place, holding more interest and possibility. My best hope was that they'd go on writing together.

When I moved to British Columbia, I contacted the continuing studies department of a local art school to see if they might be interested in offering some of the writing workshops I had offered at the Maine College of Art. The answer? A clear and resounding, No. Next I tried one of the community colleges, whose answer was an enthusiastic, Yes! We started with a daylong journal workshop, which got just enough registrants to go forward. The next one we offered was undersubscribed, so the college canceled it, even though I offered to take less money or waive my fee altogether; it was bad public relations to cancel a workshop and certainly no way to build a program and attract future registrants. But policy was policy; there were no exceptions. I began to hear from people who'd signed up for the canceled classes, asking if I offered them anywhere else. I told them if they could find a dining-room table and five to seven people, I'd do it. That's how my house workshops began, first in West Vancouver and later downtown. Once I moved to an apartment big enough for my own table, I gathered people around that.

The first meeting of a writing circle is always awkward. We're joined by the ghosts of shaming English teachers, the painfully self-conscious teenagers we once were, with a head full of rules we're both eager and afraid to break. We're acutely aware of our failings and secretly hungry for praise. All of which just sort of hangs in the air. I do what I can to dispel the cloud of gloom. We will simply follow our own thoughts and keep our pens moving. For this is not writing as we usually think of it. It's listening and gradually learning to suspend our opinions about what we hear. Before I invite people to read, I offer some simple guidelines. No comments. No feedback. Just listen—and notice what that's like.

Hearing our own voice in the listening presence of others is liberating. When we hear others read aloud, we are carried deeper together into greater empathy, wisdom, grace, spirit, and astonishing synchronicities. As we gather week after week, we write for the sheer pleasure of discovering what's on our minds. We write freed from the tyranny of objectives and desired outcomes, under the radar of Amazon and Google, and beyond even Siri's earshot. Together we explore what happens when we stay awake to ourselves, our instincts and desires. What happens if we listen, really listen to and with our bodies? How close can we come to telling the truth? What happens when we dig through the topsoil toward bedrock and the good groundwater?

I suspect there has never been a time when these questions were not dangerous. And so they are today. All the more reason to come to the table, smooth the sheet of paper before us, take pen in hand, and resume what my beloved and irascible mentor Pamela Wood used to call the sweaty work of writing.

Feeding the Ghosts of Christmas Past

Sauerkraut

Every year my mother would put a large dish of it on the sideboard along with the carved turkey and stuffing and cranberry sauce for Christmas dinner, and each of us would be obliged to have a small portion as a way of showing respect to my father's mother, her sister Florence, and their childhood friend Edwina, three ancient ladies of German descent.

My mother hated Germans, not so much because of the war but because of her mother-in-law. At best, their relations were strained. At worst, they flared into open combat. At least as open as life in a 1950s St. Louis suburb would allow. Which looked a good bit more like the subterfuge that characterized the years of the Cold War.

The root of the conflict lay in the fact that they were a great deal alike in temperament. Both had strong opinions, and neither was shy about expressing them.

Christmas being what it is, one makes an effort to be of good will, and my mother's goodwill gesture toward Grandmother each year was sauerkraut.

There was always a lot left over. Sauerkraut, that is.

Aunt Edwina survived my grandmother and Aunt Florence by a good many years, so each Christmas, my mother continued to serve sauerkraut. One year, she passed around the sauerkraut dish for second helpings, though it was clear that no one had had a first.

"Aunt Edwina?" she said, leaning over.

"No thanks," said Aunt Edwina, "I've never much cared for it myself."

I could almost read my mother's mind: If Edwina had never liked it, then what about Aunt Florence and Grandmother? All that goodwill sauerkraut for naught.

Eggnog

It's got to be the nastiest liquid on earth—a waste of perfectly good bourbon. Of course not everyone agrees, and since it's a Christmas tradition, it filled the cut-crystal punch bowl on Christmas Eve and then again on Christmas morning. My mother loved serving it to her mother-in-law and our maiden aunts, all teetotalers. After three cups or so, the old ladies would start giggling, without any clear notion of what was funny.

And my mother would grin, triumphant.

The good bourbon (Jim Beam, Old Grand-Dad, or Jack Daniel's) was prominently on display, and everyone's first highball was poured from that, but as my mother went around to freshen everybody's drink, she'd carry the glasses out to the kitchen and pour from the bottle of 905, a brand produced by the local liquor store of the same name.

Fruitcake

Speaking of bourbon, another Christmas treat that turned my stomach was fruitcake, the second-nastiest thing in the world after eggnog. To think of the two together is almost more than I can bear. But, once again, to many it is the very essence of Christmas—heavy, dense, full of candied fruit, and highly alcoholic. It was always a gift. From Mrs. Weintraub next door. And so it was also showcased, and after a few hearty souls had a thin slice or two, most of it went the route of the leftover sauerkraut.

Candy Canes and Oranges

They appeared in my Christmas stocking, and both were disappointments simply because they weren't chocolate. Even so, I remember how exotic oranges seemed. I'm not sure why, but we never had any sort of fresh fruit around, except bananas—orange juice came from frozen concentrate. Oranges on Christmas morning were intriguing because I had to peel them, they sprayed a fine mist that tickled my nose, and they didn't come out of a can. In the 1950s, that was sort of unusual. At least in our house.

In fact I don't think I actually encountered an orange on a tree until I was well into my forties on a trip to California, and—I kid you not—my first thought was: Californians are so weird, they hang ornaments on their trees in summertime.

Santa's Milk and Cookies

I can't for the life of me remember actually putting them out for Santa. It may have been one of those traditions that my family dispensed with before I was born. I was the youngest of four. I do, however, remember, my distress one year that Santa couldn't possibly come because St. Louis almost never had any snow at Christmastime. My father took pains to explain to me that for the southern route, Santa used a helicopter.

I was skeptical.

"How does he land it on a sloping roof?" I asked.

"The same way he lands his sleigh up north," said my father.

"What about the reindeer?" I asked.

"Oh they're helping to pull. Remember there's a load of presents. And they know the route better than Santa himself," my father assured me.

Everybody got the sense that year that I had outgrown Santa, and the next year, Santa didn't drop in on Christmas Eve to have a glass of Christmas cheer. (The fact that Santa drank eggnog was a mark against him in my book.) True, the two previous years, I'd had a pretty good idea who was behind the fake belly and white beard, especially the year it was my older brother, but I had played along like the good sport I was always trying to be.

I can't remember how old I was that year, but I was bereft and was working my way into a fit of tears. Whereupon my father snuck upstairs, put on one of my sister's red winter coats, managed to stick some cotton balls on his face, and came back down.

"Ho! Ho! Ho!" he roared.

"Boo! Hoo! Hoo!" I roared louder, not to be consoled by cheap tricks.

All these years later, I think: If only I'd had the presence of mind to soften, just a little. I was, in fact, too old for Santa, but I wanted the adults to keep up the illusion, so I could act like I was playing along.

If only I had appreciated the apology inherent in my father's ridiculous getup that night. If only I'd been willing, even for a moment, to believe in make-believe.

August 1974

Just before I lost consciousness, I felt tired. I wanted to rest. Only for a moment. I had been racing around like a madman all summer, trying to make up for time I had lost in a kind of nervous breakdown the previous winter. By Thanksgiving, I was overwhelmed, strung out, and failing three of the five courses I had signed up for in the fall, including a religious studies course called Witchcraft, Magic, and the Irrational. I lay on my bed upstairs at my parents' house, half convinced I had rabies, after a playful Great Dane had put his large jaws around my forearm and scratched the skin when I panicked and pulled away. The dog might have been a witch's familiar a classmate had sent out to do me harm. I was clearly out of my mind. I came to a decision. I would finish the two courses I was passing, take one incomplete, and withdraw from the other two. I would register for only two courses the following semester and get back into therapy. Crazy as I was, I knew I needed to propose something reasonable to my parents if I was to salvage what credits I could toward my BA, without which I might be trapped in St. Louis forever.

In the moment before I lost consciousness, I leaned back in my seat and closed my eyes. I wanted it to stop. All of it: running from pillar to post, to my morning class, to a bar for lunch, to another class, to the library, to my parents' house for dinner, to the library, to a bar, to a club, to another bar or someone's house for more drugs or sex, then back to my parents' house in the suburbs to sleep it off.

When I leaned back in my seat and closed my eyes, my right foot pushed the gas pedal to the floor. I was driving from St. Louis to Minneapolis to see friends after summer school. Some time off before the fall semester. A hot bright afternoon, my arm resting out the open window, the radio blasting, a can of beer between my legs, several empties strewn on the floor, a flask of tequila in the glove compartment. Free and easy on the open road. But suddenly I was very tired. I needed to rest my eyes. But just for a minute.

The impact threw me against the shoulder belt, then back again. Everything stopped. I was awake. There must have been sounds, but I don't remember hearing them. The windshield was intact, but the front of my Volkswagen Beetle had slammed shut like a squeezebox. Two people were staring at me, startled, as if I were in their backseat, which I very nearly was.

I undid my seat belt and ran to the driver's side of the car I had hit.

"Are you okay?" I called in through the window, as if I were standing at a greater distance than I was. Then everything came close, too close, as though through a zoom lens.

"Yes," said the man.

"Are you okay?" asked the woman.

"Yes," I said. "I think so."

"Are you drunk?" asked the man.

"No," I said. "I must have dozed off."

By the summer of 1974, my psyche was badly fractured. Every fault line marked a different persona, and though none had split entirely, each inclined in its own direction, away from whatever remained of my central core. A tendency, not a schism. Looking back, I had been in a prolonged state of breakdown for two years, with sharp spikes and plunges, "like a fever chart for a bad case of melancholy," as the poet Anne Sexton once put it.

In June 1972, I returned to the States from nine months in Europe—three traveling on the continent and six living in Cambridge, England, working in a bookstore.

In Amsterdam, a waiter took me home after his shift ended, changed into an embroidered silk dressing gown, and told me the story of his dead lover and the parrot he'd left him. The bird only spoke Italian, which he didn't understand. In Luxembourg, I drank all night with a slender man in a black turtleneck who had worked as a mercenary and had fallen in love with a woman in India who'd given him a sandalwood bead, whose fragrance still drove him wild with desire for something he could never have. In Florence, I began to feel parts of my body disappear as I walked along a street. I made it back to the pension, collapsed on the bed, and shivered and sweated for three days, barely able to eat, drinking sips of water and taking aspirina that a South African medical student had bought for me at the pharmacy around the corner. I recovered enough to get on the train to Paris, my last stop before heading to England. When I unlocked the door to my room in the hotel, I saw a copy of Sylvia Plath's second collection of poems, *Ariel*, lying on the bed. A sign, I thought. Of something.

Once I had settled in Cambridge, at a pub favored by my workmates, I fell in with a group of laborers, theater folk, and would-be geniuses, all highly eccentric, many of them heavy drinkers, and one or two psychiatric patients. My kind of crowd, as it turned out. Not one had anything to do with the university. I became friendly with one of the carpenters from the Arts Theatre, Rupert, who was in love with one of the psychiatric patients named Fitch, whose wife lived in a nearby town. Fitch usually came to the pub accompanied by a woman with a pale round face devoid of expression, who would stare at my box of matches, convinced it was full of razor blades.

"Oh no," I'd say, shaking and then opening the box. "Matches. See?"

Rupert fell into a serious depression. I stepped in to save him, drank with him at his place after the pub closed, and often fell into bed with him, fumbling around before we both passed out. One morning he arrived at the theater workshop with a bandaged wrist. His boss sent him to the hospital when he figured out what had happened, which, in turn, brought the police around to the bookstore because Rupert had said I would explain everything.

"Is your friend homosexual?" asked the officer. We were upstairs in the manager's office.

"Not that I know of," I said. I had only just turned twenty. I had no clear idea of what was and was not legal in England, and I didn't want either of us to end up in jail.

Not to leave you hanging, Rupert recovered and went on to a satisfying tenure at the National Theatre, retired to Norfolk, and is happily at work on still lifes and landscapes in a small studio at the bottom of his garden.

I didn't know that the story had a happy ending when I returned to the States in June after my work permit ran out. I was confused and guilt-ridden. By the time I reached St. Louis, I was in a state of shock, profoundly disoriented. People drove on the wrong side of the street. American money felt light and tinny. People's voices and accents seemed harsh and loud. And yet, at the same time, the world was muffled, somehow, at a slight remove, as if my life were happening to someone else.

My father rented an apartment for me on McCausland Avenue in a neighborhood called Dogtown, where roaming packs of stray dogs became rabid one summer and had to be gunned down. Or so the story went. I had transferred from the college I'd been attending in southern Wisconsin to Webster University outside St. Louis. Classes had not yet begun, so I sat in a wicker chair at a rolling typewriter table in the front room, trying to write a novel about whomever it was my life seemed to be happening to.

I lost no time in falling in love. This time I went for a mysterious man with long black hair and piercing Persian eyes. A poet, it turned out. He was wearing a blue seersucker suit the night he took a seat at my table in a West End bar, leaned in nose-to-nose, and said, "Do you want to get laid?"

"Sure!" I said, laughing. And he sensed his mistake. He meant did I want to team up with him in search of women. But it was too late. I was smitten. He chased women, and I chased him, reenacting Lady Caroline Lamb's hot and ridiculous pursuit of Lord Byron. Years later, a social worker explained that what I had done was called stalking. And it had nothing whatsoever to do with love.

Everything I did to escape the pain I was in only deepened and further distorted it. Nothing I did to alleviate the gnawing at my heart seemed to have any effect at all.

By the end of my second semester at Webster University, I sat immobilized in my wicker chair, staring at the sheet of paper I had rolled into the typewriter, then peering under the drawn window shade, watching traffic go by. I drank beer. I smoked cigarettes. I turned back to the typewriter. I had no will. I was breaking apart inside. Somehow, I managed to pass my college courses. At the end of May, I moved back into my parents' house, and a week or two later packed my bag. I would spend the summer with my older brother in Colorado and get myself sorted out.

I decided to drive straight through, which would have taken fifteen or sixteen hours, had I not run into a snowstorm in the Rockies. I alternated beer with coffee to keep myself awake. I found a phone booth at the Aspen Airport and stared at an old Cessna stuck tail up in the mud, a joke or a genuine crash, I never found out. My brother finally answered.

"I wasn't expecting you till tomorrow," he said.

"I know. I drove straight through."

"But there was a snowstorm. They closed the pass."

"It wasn't closed when I came over."

"You're crazy," he said, sounding genuinely concerned.

"We both know that. Now tell me how to get to your house."

He was the caretaker for a property in an exclusive development about twenty minutes north of Aspen. It didn't take us long to figure out that living together that summer wasn't going to work, so I moved to Independence Lodging, essentially a rooming house, which, according to legend, had been a brothel during the gold rush. A three-story red-brick building with storefronts at street level, the top two stories had rooms around an open gallery with a balcony rail forming a large U. Two squeaky metal cots to a room. Communal showers and toilets. My roommate was a tall lanky pothead named Roy. I got a job washing dishes, which provided me with a meal and all the beer I could drink on my shift, a perk that was meant to make up for the fact I took no share in the tips. I divided my time between getting high with Roy in our room, working at the restaurant, stopping by an A-frame breakfast place where we bought our dope, and attending lectures and master classes at the Aspen Music Festival and

School of Music, where a friend of mine from high school studied opera each summer. And I read—the *Diaries* of Anaïs Nin, Lawrence Durrell's *The Alexandria Quartet,* Diane Wakoski's *Inside the Blood Factory,* and anything else I could find at the Unicorn bookstore.

One afternoon just as I'd finished smoking a joint, there was a knock on the door and a voice announcing the FBI. I froze and waved a towel up and down to get rid of the cloud of smoke. I opened the door. The agent said he was looking for Roy, actually Roy's brother, to see if he could identify a woman associated with the Weather Underground. I told him that Roy wasn't in, but I'd be happy to look at the photos to see if I recognized her. My thought went something like this: If I did recognize anyone, I would say nothing and heroically turn the page. Of course I didn't recognize anyone in the photos, which was a little disappointing. I wanted to do something, however small, to further the aims of the revolution. The truth was, I was too damaged, too engrossed in my own lunacy to be of any serious interest to revolutionaries or the police.

At summer's end, I drove back to St. Louis to start another semester of college, the one I ended up not finishing. The following January, I met with a new therapist, who, when I explained why I was taking only two courses, drawing and French, joked: "So. You're going to be a French artist." It stung, but I didn't take offense. He was only trying to lift the very dark cloud I was under. My hunch is that he sensed the real danger I was in. And yet I don't remember him ever asking about my drinking or drug use, though more often than not I would arrive at his office stoned and read to him from my journals, which were all about chasing the dark poet from bar to bar and the people I encountered and slept with along the way. Or maybe it was just 1974. Alcohol—even heavy drinking—was a normal part of life in a culture where coming-of-age meant learning how to drink if not responsibly, at least respectably. It was trial and error. Some errors were more costly than others. In spite of it all, it must have seemed to my therapist that I was making progress toward a more stable and functional life. Maybe it even seemed so to me.

Once I knew that the couple in the car I had hit were okay, I ran around to the passenger side of my own car, opened the door, and started tossing empty beer cans over my shoulder. The police would be there soon. Though it was long before mobile phones, it was not before radar on interstate highways. I had to have a story. I would tell them I picked up a hitchhiker. The beer was his. He offered me one, so I drank it. Just one. It was a hot day, after all. Then I let him out. He was the one who drank all the other beers. Not me. A hitchhiker, then. He had ridden with me for a while. I don't remember how long, long enough to drink five or six beers. The flask of tequila in the glove compartment was his too. Where did I leave him? He got out at the last exit. I picked him up early in the morning. Just outside St. Louis.

A police cruiser pulled up, lights flashing. One officer went to talk to the couple in the Buick. The other one asked me questions, his notebook open.

"No sir, only one. Yes sir, at the last exit. Yes sir, the tequila was his too."

The officer said nothing to contradict me, though he knew I was lying. I knew he knew, and yet that's the story I had to tell. He read me my rights. He asked me to stretch my arms out from the shoulder and then touch my nose with my right index finger and then the left. He had me walk in a straight line first one way and then had me turn around and walk back. He asked me if I'd be willing to take a breathalyzer test, explaining that refusing to do so was an admission of guilt. I took my chances. I failed it.

He asked me if I was going to be sick.

I said no.

"All right then," he said, "get into the car."

I collected my suitcase and my backpack and got into the backseat of the police car. We waited for his partner to finish taking statements from the couple in the Buick, and they drove on.

The sheriff's office was bright and clean—also air-conditioned. The officer allowed me two phone calls—one to my parents and the other to my friends in Minneapolis. He booked me on charges of drunk driving, and then escorted me to one of the cells in back. I was the only one in jail that day in Cameron, Missouri. I lay down on the hard bed, peered through the bars for a moment, and then passed out. I slept, waking with a start every so often, wondering where I was, cotton-mouthed, thirsty, dehydrated. The next morning, another officer drove me to the Greyhound Bus Station. My red VW Beetle was undrivable. A total wreck.

The bus ride back to St. Louis was long—but not long enough. I dreaded having to face my parents at the other end of it. I rehearsed my story about the hitchhiker, my poor judgment, the lessons I had learned, as if I were heading into the end of an episode of *Leave It to Beaver.* Every part of my body ached and felt injured. I was too scared to let myself know how scared I really was. I could only just graze the edge of my shame.

Later, it rose in me, hot and dark, each time I had to tell the story to the lawyer my father hired or the insurance agent who lived next door. I heard myself tell the story as if I were a distant relative of the driver but close enough to feel mortified.

Me and not me. That's how I experienced myself—or selves—in those years. I would stand outside the door of Duff's restaurant on North Euclid, deciding who I was going to be when I stepped across the threshold: spurned lover of a poet, comrade of Trotskyists, trusted friend of lesbians, misplaced Beatnik folk hero. Not a masquerade so much as a show where one actor plays all the roles, morphing right before your eyes—like magic.

Weeks later an envelope arrived from the Missouri State Police with a Polaroid of my wrecked car. I thought it looked funny, the front slammed shut like a crushed beer can, but it sent a shiver up my spine. My mother took one look, turned the picture over on the kitchen table, and pushed it away.

The sight of my wrecked car was more than she could bear. As unhinged and disconnected as I was at the time, I felt I had to protect her and my father, who was by then a late-stage alcoholic. The truth about me might reveal too much about them. We were all committed to upholding a delusion of normal, even if it cost us our lives.

"Do you think you wanted to die?" asked my therapist at our next session.

"I don't know," I said.

It hadn't occurred to me to want to die. I just wanted—something indistinct, elusive, out there somewhere. The right course of study. The right mode of expression. The right lover. A way to safety. I had come unmoored, been set adrift. I had fallen out of meaning into a two-dimensional world and was in danger of falling off the edge. Instead, I had run into the back of a Buick in broad daylight on a bone-dry stretch of highway, dead drunk.

Later that fall, Anne Sexton died. A friend read the article in *Time*. Sexton had put on her mother's fur coat, poured herself a glass of vodka, gone into the garage, started the car—and waited. When I saw my therapist later that day, I sat silent in the chair for a long time. I started to tell him about Sexton, but when I tried to speak, my throat filled with acid and bile. I ran to the washroom down the hall and was violently sick. I came back into the office, shaken, pale, and clammy.

"It must be the flu," I said.

I had a few sips of water and then drove home.

Like John Berryman, Robert Lowell, and Sylvia Plath, Sexton had captured, reflected, and helped to shape the fascination with madness that was so much a part of that era. Reading Plath in college led me to Sexton's first collection, *To Bedlam and Part Way Back.* As brilliant and shocking as Plath's poems were, Sexton's poems lingered with me and worked their way under my skin. She seemed to have a more robust life and there was in her work glimmers of hope, a pulse of light—not Plath's "blood jet." I found in Sexton a fellow traveler, a pilgrim in search of God, who had not yet lost touch with "the sun, / the dream, the excitable gift."

As I lost consciousness on that hot bright August afternoon on Interstate 35 heading north toward Minneapolis, I could feel myself begin to lift out of my body, turning to leave, even as my right foot pushed the gas pedal to the floor. "Oh no, you don't," said my body. For something else was at work. Something else had taken over—a benevolent force, an angel, Sophia, the Holy Spirit—something had acted through my body and made it clear I was not going anywhere. God was not finished with me yet.

The following spring, I passed my comprehensive exams and earned my BA in English literature. I had also been awarded a teaching assistantship and would be leaving for northern France in the fall. After the graduation ceremony, I found my parents outside. My mother wore a bright yellow dress and sunglasses. My father's gray suit hung on his emaciated body. He had just been released from what would turn out to be his last alcohol rehabilitation program. He looked pale, drawn, and worried. But he was sober and would remain so for the rest of his life.

I still had another decade or so of what I thought of as controlled drinking—panic attacks, compulsive work, dangerous lapses of memory, and anxiety-ridden love affairs.

Nevertheless, something had shifted.

I had decided to live.

The Enigma of Healing

Influenza. A musical word, like belladonna. Beguiling, and potentially fatal. From the Italian word for "influence," suggesting an unfavorable alignment of stars. Better known by its pet name "flu," it's the thing we hope to avoid each winter. Shot or no shot, it can enter our lives through the air we breathe, the hands we shake, or the poles we grab to keep from falling over when the bus lurches forward or comes to a sudden stop.

It's ubiquitous. Like fear.

And despite my best efforts and massive doses of vitamin C, it took me down in January 2013, with subtle hints at first and then with real insistence. Before I knew it, I was down for the count. I canceled everything in my daybook for the following two weeks and went back to bed, where I surrendered to fevered delirium, fitful sleep, and waking dreams—nightmares mostly—of my life in various stages of collapse.

Six weeks earlier in yet another windowless hotel conference room, I discovered what I already knew: I was bored stupid by training corporate trainers and consultants.

Now my body ached all over. Fiery tendrils radiated out of my tailbone and down my legs, whether I lay on my back or on my side. The only relief I found was standing in a hot shower. I'd leave one of the window blinds open each night, so I could look out and see lights in other buildings, other people awake at three and four in the morning. I was confronted again and again by the wide variety of my failings: venomous student evaluations when I was still teaching, botched love affairs, mediocre reviews, abysmal book sales, any number of unfinished projects abandoned, disappointing everyone's expectations, including my own.

Just as I was beginning to hope I might be listed among the fatalities of the flu outbreak, the fever broke, and I woke up in a T-shirt drenched with sweat, curious and bemused. For I had woken up in someone else's life; whoever had lived before me in this place was dead, and I was giddy with relief. I knew what I had to do: resign from any number of jobs I had taken on, and pick up strands of my life I had let drop. It was like stripping a room bare, then deciding, one object at a time, what I wanted to put back in it.

Slowly, deliberately, I entered something I would one day call my new life.

I grew up in a family beset by chronic illness. My father suffered from a host of indefinable ills and was generally thought to be a hypochondriac. Within the span of one year, my older brother came down with what doctors at first thought was spinal meningitis, and the younger of my two elder sisters began suffering from intestinal maladies that mystified our family physician. My mother and I spent a lot of time in hospital waiting rooms during those months. I tried doing homework and she leafed through magazines she had already read and lit one cigarette off of another, while we waited for physicians who told us that the tests showed nothing conclusive other than my father worried too much, that he needed to learn how to relax, put on some weight, get some fresh air, maybe take up golf, or that the good news was what ailed my brother was double pneumonia and not meningitis, and that my sister should probably change her diet and not drink so much Coca-Cola. My mother did her best to reassure me that everything was going to be all right, but it was clear she suspected that nothing was going to be all right ever again. Indeed, the hospitalizations and evenings in the waiting rooms continued for years.

Illness hung over our house like bad air over a swamp. It more and more defined us to the outside world as well as inside the family. Some of us were ill; others were not. To be ill meant something was wrong with you. A physician's job was to give it a name and make it go away. Illness was supposed to be temporary, and that it lingered gave rise to misgivings about the rightness of our lives, our goodness, and our virtue. For years I watched members of my family grow more and more isolated and stigmatized as a result of their illness. Again and again I had to learn to accept my powerlessness and to love them as best I could through my own pain as a witness to their suffering.

Illness has long been seen as a result of wrongdoing or wrong living, the result of bad habits, poor choices. Illness carries with it an onus of guilt and shame. Why me? What have I done to incur the displeasure and punishment of the gods? Whether it's maraschino cherries, aluminum cookware, lead-based paint and asbestos in an old house, a melancholic nature, negative thinking, something has caused the illness and we struggle to find out what it means and what will effect a cure.

When my friend Rick was diagnosed with lung cancer, I wasn't just shocked, I was dumbfounded. No one I knew had a healthier lifestyle. He lived in a rural area, was a massage therapist, practiced yoga, maybe had an occasional glass of wine. And he didn't smoke! As I prayed that he would make a full recovery, I realized that somehow I had it in mind that meant he would be restored to his former state of excellent health as if the cancer had never occurred. An absurd notion, but there it was. A belief about recovery that was being challenged by my own experience with a twelve-step program, which involved a radical shift in my relationship to the condition, not its eradication. This was not a war or a fight I was going to "win"; in fact my recovery began with and depended upon my surrender to an ongoing healing process, which was, to be sure, a return to health, but not without being profoundly changed by the illness itself. It did not and could never mean I would be "as good as new"—yet how many of us hold that view and to what extent do physicians themselves have this as their aim, however unconscious it may be?

The centaur Chiron from Greek mythology has become emblematic of the wounded healer. Abandoned by his mother, Chiron was taken in by Apollo and, under his tutelage, became a physician and mentor to such heroes as Achilles. There are a number of different versions of the story of his wounding. One recounts that an arrow meant for someone else accidently landed in Chiron's body. He could neither find a way to heal the wound nor die from it because, as a demigod, he was immortal. In her book, *Chiron and The Healing Journey,* astrologer and cosmologist Melanie Reinhart is quick to point out that "Chiron's wound is not his 'fault.'" She goes on to say, "Chiron's process is not about the diagnosis and description of pathology, but concerns how we relate to our experience, and what we 'make of it.'"

Remember that Chiron has a dual nature, half horse/half human, and holds the dynamic tension between animal instinct and human consciousness. What's more, it is through his wound that he gains greater wisdom, which he then passes on to others—indeed his healing power rests in the wound itself. The wound in this case is an initiation. Essential to the healing process is finding—often at long last—some measure of grace in the original wound, which in turn, seems to open us to deeper levels of transformative power. In order to do this, one has to enter the wound, experience it and all the emotions that arise from it: outrage, grief, guilt, blame, betrayal, and whatever else it may contain. Healers are often drawn to healing practice through their own wounds or those of family members. The unhealable wound becomes characteristic of all healing—a paradox indeed.

Healing is a mystery we enter into with someone else. In a very real sense, the relationship does the work, not just the physician/practitioner or the one who seeks healing. Desire, will, and readiness are key. Healing happens on more than one level—body, heart, and soul. Twelve-steppers describe recovery from alcoholism as a threefold process: physical, emotional, and spiritual. In 2013, when my fever broke from my bout of influenza, I once again realized that I had to change every aspect of my life.

Illness grabs our attention physically first. As alcohol was cycling out of my body, I found myself in front of the candy shelves or staring into the ice-cream freezer at the grocery story. At the time I wasn't eating candy or ice cream, but now I was tormented by cravings. Friends and my physician explained that my body was looking to replace the sugar supply it had lost when I stopped drinking. The advice from friends in AA was to just go for the substitution at this early stage of my sobriety. I could work with my sugar addiction later on.

When I quit drinking, I also noticed I was in physical pain. My left shoulder and neck felt pinched and were unbearably tight. A friend recommended a chiropractor. I was skeptical, having grown up hearing they were quacks, but painkillers were not an option, so I called the guy. When he gave my head a quick jerk and I heard the pops and crunches, I thought for sure he'd broken my neck, but when I got up from the table, I could move my head without constriction. I was sore, but not in the pain I'd been in before. When I got home, I lay down and promptly fell asleep for a few hours, a response that someone later explained was quite natural since I was releasing. What and how I was releasing, I had no idea. I just let it happen, surrendering to one part of the healing process and then the next.

Chiropractic adjustments brought my spine into alignment, but my muscles remembered the old pattern and kept pulling the spine back into familiar territory. Which led me to a massage therapist, which in turn brought up body image and the extent to which all touch had become sexualized in me. But my first awareness was that massage was helping me to hold my chiropractic adjustment and drawing my attention to how I was walking, sitting, and swimming. I became aware of muscle memory outside of the mechanical functions of posture, and movement. Apparently, muscle tissue also carried emotion. The grief and sadness and fear stored in muscles sometimes got released in massage, resulting in what seemed like inexplicable tears. Now and then, I could point to specific events, which got activated once the muscle was palpated or the holding spasm was released. But just as often their origin was a mystery to me.

A five-day retreat devoted to family dynamics and the release of suppressed emotion opened me up about as wide as I'd ever been. I didn't want to close back down, so I started getting acupuncture. I wasn't seeking relief from any specific symptom, but wanted to keep my energy field open without really understanding what that meant. Less clinical than traditional Chinese medicine, Worsley Classical Five-Element Acupuncture seemed just the thing. And it was—for me at least—largely because of Tom, the acupuncturist. Instinct and intuition were coming alive in me again, and following them, I encountered healing practitioners who were themselves attuned to intuition and energy awareness. I didn't really understand much about what he was doing other than sticking needles into my body and unblocking energy pathways. Sometimes I felt an electrical charge or shock or a dull sinking ache when the energy moved. Tom's way of practicing retained many of the metaphorical and metaphysical elements that have somehow gotten lost along the way in TCM. Each point had a name, an image. Prince's Grandson pointed to lineage and the future. People Welcome suggested inward and outward flowing movement, which came to mind as I prepared my table for dinner guests.

It became clear to me that no single intervention was going to do the trick—relieve symptoms and restore my equilibrium. I was confronted with age-old questions about how the body, emotions, spirit, and soul were related. Where did illness come from? How did it travel? How did it pattern itself? Unbeknownst to me, I had somehow set out to explore how all this worked. And as I was to find out, any call to healing is a call into dangerous territory. For most, if not everything, we now hold as accepted practice began somewhere in the margins—or over the edge—of conventional thought. The pioneering inquires of early practitioners often cost them their lives. There was a lot at stake, and sometimes the stake was a burning one.

I decided to study massage. There were two schools to choose from. One offered good, solid, clinically based programs in therapeutic and sports massage in a town about a forty-minute drive away. The other, though based in Ipswich, Massachusetts, offered classes in Portland, Maine, where I was living, and had classes not only in Swedish massage but also gave certification in polarity therapy, an energy-based healing modality developed by Dr. Randolph Stone. It was the focus on energy of the Polarity Realization Institute that finally persuaded me. And yet, almost from the beginning, I feared I'd made a mistake. I was surrounded by New Age ninnies in white clothes, talking in breathy voices, and wearing amethyst pendants and earrings. I was one of the only men.

Luckily my two favorite instructors were Yankee women with common sense, a healthy skepticism, and a sense of humor.

In the polarity model, energy steps down into matter, becoming denser in each element—from the etheric realm, through air, fire, water, and then earth. The idea was that illness began in the energy field and descended into the body. Could it not, I wondered, move the other way? Say, begin in an organ and step up and out into the energy field. And how did all this stepping down or up take place? Not all the teachers welcomed my questions—but the ones I learned the most from were fellow researchers, learning as they practiced, in much the same way Dr. Stone had. We were pioneers in the unseen world. And more often than not, I was the one who got lost.

Our first workshop on using crystals began with a review of how they focused, intensified, and directed energy. Then we went over how to clear the chakras and auric field. We divided into pairs to practice. I opened the energy cavities in the body before placing a small crystal on my partner's third eye and a larger one at the heart center. Then I added one at the base of the throat, the solar plexus, the second chakra, a spot between the navel and the pubic bone and one at the root chakra below that. So far so good. I noticed others were removing the crystals, so I figured it was time to do that.

Then came clearing the chakras by pointing the tip of my crystal at the energy center, starting at the crown, and drawing the energy up and away from the body to open the channel and clear anything that might be clogging the energy. Clear them of what, you might ask. I was told to think of it as smoke or dark spots, though I couldn't see them. I just imitated the sweeping gestures I saw others making with their arms up and away from each chakra, proceeding toward the root. So far, so good.

When it came time to clear the layers of the aura, I was flummoxed. I couldn't tell which layer I was in, where one layer began and another stopped. Others in the class had already described their astonishing ability to see auras and colors and which way a chakra was spinning. I saw nothing and stood there, crystal in hand, utterly lost. The instructor came over and asked if anything was wrong.

"I can't see anything," I said. "I have no idea where to begin."

"Ah," she said. "Nothing to worry about. Not everybody gets the information visually. Use your imagination. Begin where you think the first layer is, close to the body, and drag your crystal through it slowly. If you feel the tug of something, pull it out of the field and drop it into an etheric burning ground." Which of course I also couldn't see and had to imagine. I tried it, and I began to feel a tug here and there in one layer and then in another, but not in every layer.

Our debriefing after lunch focused on different ways of seeing, sensing, feeling, and imagining—each an important part of the work we were learning. We were already working with something that most people had little or no awareness of—energy fields, centers, and pathways—so in that sense we were ahead of the game. I could feel something shift in me. I could trust my intuition and imagination, a felt sense in the body, not just what I was seeing, which widened the range of my awareness in healing work in ways I already trusted implicitly as a writer and teacher.

I began to see the key role that imagination was playing in my own healing process. When Jesus asks people if they want to be healed, I hear another implied question: Are you willing to be changed? And that depends in large part on my ability to imagine that I can be different. The work of the imagination often begins below the level of waking consciousness. New images begin to form, sensations, inklings of how I might feel, who I might be on the other side of this illness. All forms of healing involve becoming conscious of what has been unconscious and are therefore dangerous because they challenge ways we have seen ourselves and the beliefs and opinions we have formed about the world. One remembers the resistance faced by such controversial figures as Ida Rolf, Elisabeth Kübler-Ross, and Wilhelm Reich, all of whom in some way explored how physiology, thought, imagination, and energy work together in mysterious ways that seem fluid, organic, and well beyond our notions of cause and effect. Carl Jung talked a great deal about synchronicity. Events coincide, seem unrelated, and yet come into relationship with each other, opening us to new experiences and understanding.

Most healing practitioners and allopathic physicians agree that their primary task is to help the body heal itself, to restore balance or homeostasis, and to support the natural course of healing. And if that sounds unscientific, it's because it is, at least in the way many have come to understand and describe how science works, which, of course, is undergoing rapid and radical change, opening new vistas and areas of research, as well as very old ways of knowing, which don't necessarily contradict one another but which are nonetheless hard to square with ideas handed down to us from the Enlightenment. Everywhere I see physicians, botanists, psychologists, biologists, pathologists, physicists, philosophers, and theologians exploring the territories created by overlapping fields of study, bodies of knowledge, and ways of knowing.

When I moved to Vancouver from Maine, I naturally considered which parts of my life and work I could transplant and which parts I needed to toss onto the compost heap. My professional life focused more and more on supporting and developing leaders in nonprofits and the public sector through my work as an executive coach. I set my healing practice to one side and got busy with survival in a city where my living expenses were much higher than they'd been back East. I had to drum up business—a lot of it, and fast. I was stepping into a narrower professional identity without fully realizing what I was losing by sloughing off the old one. While I was getting settled, I attended a lecture with friends. As we talked at the back of the auditorium before the lecture began, a man my friends knew asked if I did spiritual work. "Not so's you'd notice," I quipped. It ended the conversation, and I felt bad. Later, we found ourselves at the same restaurant, and I had a chance to apologize, explaining that the question had thrown me and that I hadn't meant to be rude. What I didn't say because I didn't yet know it myself was how deeply unsettling the question was to me. I have, in fact, been doing undercover spiritual work all my life—in my family, at school, as a teacher, bookseller, writer, social worker, polarity therapist, and, yes, even as an executive leadership coach. For a complete stranger to somehow see that about me was unnerving. I felt exposed, betrayed, outed as a covert spiritual operative. I had no real idea how deep this conflict was in me and how out of balance my life would need to become for me to see the need for radical readjustment. My case of flu in the winter of 2013 did the trick.

The coronavirus outbreak of 2020 called me even deeper into healing—my own and that of the collective. Even before it was officially named a pandemic, I sensed the presence of the god Pan, from whom we derive the word "panic." Though his death, as recorded by Plutarch, was announced by a sailor who had heard it from a divine voice calling from across the water, it was clear to me that Pan was alive and afoot in the world once again—in the form of people's runaway fear and a sense of worldwide chaos. I'd felt his presence all too often as the twentieth century drew to its close, glimpsed him standing in the wings, ready at any moment to take center stage once again.

No one seemed to know exactly what it was, this virus, or how it traveled. It was invisible and everywhere. Fear might well have been its primary carrier. In the early days of lockdown, I took cautious walks in a nearby forest, wondering if trees had it or if dogs could spread it or insects or ferns or mold spores. The world itself seemed to have become infected, a source of contagion—poisoned. A part of me recognized this as just plain crazy. Another part of me was very nearly paralyzed. I knew I had to keep on walking, maintaining distance from others, but sure to make eye contact. It was March, then April, and spring was opening up around me. Trees were not dying, dogs seemed healthy and doglike. The world was once again coming to life. Yes, I was in the grip of fear, but if I managed to stay conscious, I could keep moving. The air was thick with anxiety, and because I am particularly susceptible to taking on other people's stuff, I couldn't shop in my usual grocery store in an underground mall. I went several blocks down the road to a larger store with high ceilings. And it wasn't the virus in the air that concerned me as much as the anxiety in the energy field. I didn't want to add my own dread to the general distress when I went out into the world. So I made sure I never left the house without first clearing as much fear as I could from my body.

I greeted everyone I met along the way, if only to make eye contact over our masks. Some stopped to exchange a few words about how we were doing. One elderly woman said no one in her building had talked to her in weeks, not even in the elevator. A building manager I had a nodding acquaintance with broke down in tears, so I held him for a time there on the sidewalk, even though we were only supposed to touch elbows. Whatever else the coronavirus was doing, it was opening up wounds from the past—weekly, daily—and our job was to heal each crisis as it emerged from within and without. It was relentless—and thorough.

Self-care became my focus and the focus of those I was working with, many of whom were themselves working with frontline physicians and nurses, social workers, psychotherapists, counselors, and allied healing practitioners. The first order of business was to decrease our own levels of stress before working with those whose stress levels were off the charts. When under this amount of strain, individuals—indeed whole organizations and countries—lose access to their resources, seem to forget the simplest and most basic ways of calming down and reregulating. In short we all go unconscious and switch to automatic pilot, fueled by adrenaline—for days, weeks, even months—until we crash.

But there was something else, another dimension to all of this. People often describe the veil between the seen and unseen worlds becoming thin around Halloween. In the early days of the pandemic, for me at least, it seemed to disappear altogether, the portal between the worlds remained wide open, and I had easier access to the ancestral realm than usual. My instinct and intuition not only grew more and more finely tuned, they were more deeply rooted in my body—working together and not at odds with each other. And it seemed I couldn't help but surrender—daily, moment by moment—to a power greater than myself, call it what you will: God, Great Spirit, Creator, Universe. That too was undergoing a radical alteration. My "concept" of God was shattering, and as I stepped more fully into the heart of creation, divine imagination itself seemed to step closer to me. Gradually, often painfully, and then with a sense of welcome relief, I noticed there was less and less difference between me and what I had always thought of as "nature." Indeed the clear distinction I held between the natural world and human nature became blurred and often dissolved altogether.

A friend who was undergoing treatment for cancer shared her dream with me: She stands near to where the waters meet, an estuary in the north, where Native peoples gather for healing ceremonies. Then she is walking into a forest. She takes off her backpack and sets it by the side of the trail. Farther on, she stops to take off her shoes and proceeds barefoot through the forest's understory. She stands still and listens. It's as if the trees are singing to her, but it's more like a hum, not really something she can hear—then she understands that she is surrounded by various high-frequency sound vibrations, each coming from a different kind of tree, and that's how the medicinal quality of each species enters her energy field and her body.

She comes to a frozen pond or a lake, a bright white oval with snow on the opposite bank, and there on the other side stands a woman of regal bearing, a shining presence. The woman across the lake wants my friend to know she's with her. And there's nothing to fear.

Bardo, Texas

It was a stand-alone funeral parlor, not one in a strip mall. What I remember is the plush carpet, soft music piped in over the shush of air-conditioning, and a whiff of chemical freshener. The windows were just for show, an architectural reference to a time when they actually opened to the outside world. It was late May. I had flown in from Maine the day before and was in the usual state of culture shock I experienced each time I came to Dallas, made even stranger by grief. I knew my favorite sister Carol was dead, but large areas of my mind remained unconvinced, even though we had been expecting this for months, even years.

Carol first became ill the summer before her seventeenth birthday. Her stomach hurt and she suffered from intense bouts of diarrhea. A bug, we thought. But the longer it went on, the more our family physician suspected something serious. What followed were years of specialists, hospitalizations, surgeries, and diagnoses—ileitis, gastroenteritis, colitis, Crohn's disease—and yet the abdominal pain, vomiting, bowel obstruction, exhaustion, and chronic weight loss continued, undiminished by treatment.

Carol's partner, Pam, had already taken care of most of the funeral details. Together they had decided everything, down to the pantsuit Carol wanted to be cremated in—one she took with her when she visited St. Louis, our mother having fixed ideas about what you wore in public. It had been a good many years since Carol had worn a skirt, much less a dress, so a pantsuit was about as fancy as she got. She kept trying to explain to our mother that Texas just wasn't as formal as St. Louis.

"Surely nobody shows up at the Junior League in blue jeans."

"Of course not, Mother. But I don't happen to belong to the Junior League."

"And that was one of your biggest mistakes when you moved to Dallas."

An argument they had been having for thirty-five years.

Carol had followed her husband to Dallas after their St. Louis wedding in October 1970. He drove the U-Haul truck with some furniture, their wedding silver, two sets of English bone china (one formal, the other for everyday use), Irish linens with her new monogram, an epergne (being a large centerpiece with branches supporting holders for candles, flowers, or sweetmeats), and a dozen Waterford crystal finger bowls for those long dinners, where guests need to freshen their hands with lemon water between courses. Carol drove her own car packed with whatever wouldn't fit in the truck.

Somehow, somewhere between Joplin, Missouri, and Tulsa, Oklahoma, they managed to run into each other. Not head-on, of course, they were both traveling south. Most likely one sideswiped the other while trying to pass or one backed into the other at a filling station. It wasn't serious, no one was hurt, but it proved a bad omen for the marriage, which ended in an acrimonious divorce five years later.

At that time, Carol suffered a debilitating recurrence of Crohn's, triggered, no doubt, by the stress of trying to get through nursing school in the middle of a divorce, never mind coming to terms with her love for women.

I don't remember how Carol and Pam met, but they fell in love while watching the Pittsburgh Steelers defeat the Los Angeles Rams in the 1980 Super Bowl. That's what they marked as their anniversary. A year or two later, Carol moved into Pam's house in Plano, a rural community that had grown into a sprawling Dallas suburb after World War II. A strange place that called to mind the unsettling peace and stability of a Twilight Zone episode. No matter how closely I followed Pam's directions, I'd get lost once I entered the parallel universe of Plano. I could not for the life of me pick out any landmarks. Each street looked pretty much the same, the houses all variations of three or four styles—split-level stockbroker Tudor, split-level French Provincial, something that looked like Greek Revival, and an upgraded version of the good old Texas split-level ranch—which repeated themselves in different patterns into infinity.

In 1982 the teen suicide rate in Plano was more than double the national average, second only to Phoenix, Arizona. Somehow that made sense to me. There was a curious deadness to the place, not quite of this world and yet not wholly of the other. A realm between death and rebirth, what the Buddhists call bardo.

"Oh," said my mother when she entered the funeral home, "this is very nice." She sounded surprised. The decor suggested Louis XIV, but stopped short of what my mother called "Jewish."

Pam led the funeral director over to us.

"Vern Abernathy," he said, taking my mother's hand in his. "I am so sorry for your loss. It is a particular affliction for a mother to lose her child."

"It most certainly is," said my mother. "Thank you."

"And you must be Carol's sister," he said turning to Ann. "I can see the resemblance."

I didn't dare look at Pam. We both knew the only way he'd ever seen Carol was dead.

"And you must be Carol's little brother." He gave me a hungry look, like I just might be lunch. Then he took Pam by the elbow.

"Y'all will excuse us for a moment." He steered her toward a rubber tree beside one of the tall windows that didn't open.

"Who is doing the service?" my mother asked me.

"They wanted their friend Harvey to do it, but he wasn't available."

"What denomination is Harvey?"

I doubted he had a denomination. Carol knew him through the gay group of Alcoholics Anonymous downtown. They'd been friends for twenty years. He cut their hair.

"I don't know. Some kind of Methodist, maybe."

The funeral director brought over a heavyset man with a hangdog face.

"This is Reverend Bob," he said. "He'll be doing the graveside service."

Later Pam told me she'd given him strict instructions: "You so much as mention Jesus, and you'll wish you'd never been born." And she meant it.

We each shook hands with Reverend Bob as he offered his condolences.

"And what denomination are you?" asked my mother.

The pastor gave her a quizzical look, as if he weren't used to being asked, much less in the tone of voice that my mother had used.

"I'm what you call an itinerant preacher, ma'am. I don't have a church of my own. I help out where I'm needed."

"That's nice," said my mother.

We'd been raised with a bland but enlightened Protestantism that stressed ethics and good manners. We considered ourselves modern and saw nothing contradictory between the book of Genesis and the theory of evolution. We abhorred Baptists and Catholics, whom we saw as unnecessarily extreme. By the time Carol and I got to Alcoholics Anonymous, we both bristled at the number of times the word God appeared in the Steps and Traditions. And we were both greatly comforted by AA's Tradition Three, which states that the only membership requirement is "a desire to stop drinking." Period. Eventually, both she and I came to believe in a power greater than ourselves. She called her higher power Gracie, after the comedian Gracie Allen.

Pam drew me aside.

"I want you to do something for me. I want you to put Carol's AA medallion in the coffin with her."

"I thought she wanted to be cremated," I said.

"She did, Alfred. But in the end I just couldn't bring myself to do it."

Carol died two days shy of her twenty-second sobriety anniversary, and as is the custom in AA, members usually celebrate by picking up a chip or coin to commemorate their time in sobriety. Whenever Carol's health allowed, she and Pam attended the annual Big D Roundup in a hotel downtown over the Memorial Day weekend. They'd rent a room, so they didn't have to drive back and forth from Plano to Dallas. I had been able to attend with them three times. It was boisterous, funny, poignant, outrageous—over-the-top in the exuberant gay Texas tradition.

"Sure," I said, despite my queasiness about seeing a dead body, much less touching one. It was right and fitting, of course, since Carol and I had accompanied each other in sobriety for twenty years and both celebrated our sobriety dates in May.

The funeral director escorted me into a back room, where Carol lay in her coffin. He undid the bolts using a hand crank and lifted the lid. Then he bowed slightly and left. There we were for one last time in the same room. I was speechless. Not empty. Not exactly at peace. It felt more like exhaustion and something akin to relief. She had been ill for so many years, had suffered so much, had been so brave and sassy and generous, despite bouts of unrelenting pain. And now it was over.

Carol had chosen her green pantsuit. It would have been fine had she been cremated as she'd requested, but it was the wrong shade if your face was a waxen yellowish hue. As it was, the pantsuit—most likely a polyester blend—would probably outlast the husk of her body underground and remain long after her great spirit had set off on its next adventure. I recalled the story of the three Taoist Laughing Masters. Just before dying one tells the others to bury him in the clothes he is wearing and not the traditional winding-sheet. It isn't clear why until they light the funeral pyre and discover he had firecrackers in his pocket.

I slipped her AA medallion under her folded hands—or what had once been her hands but were no longer. I leaned in to kiss her cold forehead and said goodbye to my first and truest friend in this life. The expression on the face she had left behind was clearly pissed off. We hadn't followed her last wishes.

"It wasn't my decision," I whispered. "It was Pam's."

Once back in the room we'd been assigned for our reception, I found two groups. One was made up of the women who worked with Pam at the pathology lab. They stood clustered together looking up at a screen on which there was a slide show. An image of Carol lying in the grass, her arms around our family dog, Lady; an image of a nine-year-old Carol standing on a dock in Wisconsin, her hair cut short and a grin full of crooked teeth; an image of her around the same age, in a football jersey that was too big for her, running a canister of water off the field with her best friend and fellow water boy, Jeannie.

"Oh look!" cried one of the women. "Doesn't she look pretty!"

The image showed Carol in a sleeveless white ball gown with an eight-foot train the color of dried blood. She wore elbow-length white kid gloves and held a massive bouquet of red roses. On her head was placed a diamond-and-sapphire-studded tiara, topped by a single egret feather. Our mother had hired somebody to paint over the photograph with tiny brushes to make it look like an oil portrait. Coming home drunk from a party one night, Carol had smashed it against the fireplace. My parents could not calm her down, so they called the family physician who arrived with a hypodermic needle.

"I didn't know she was a debutante!" said the pathology lab woman.

The other group of women stood at some distance from the first group. These were the women Pam and Carol knew from the gay bars and later from AA and Al-Anon. They looked uneasy. Pam had been every bit as clear with them as she had been with the pastor. If anybody so much as used the word lesbian in a sentence, they were dead meat.

No Jesus. No lesbians. Period.

Never mind that she and Carol had lived together for twenty-five years. It was Carol's expressed wish that no one besides me in the family know that she was a lesbian. And she had good reason. Because of her illness, she was unable to work and had been on disability for a number of years. Our mother paid her health insurance premiums each month, and without her help, she lost access to anything like adequate health care. Carol lived in fear of being cut off, and since our mother was, let's say, unpredictable and perfectly capable of doing just that as a sign of her displeasure, the fear was real.

Twelve years earlier, I'd had a panicked call from Pam.

"Alfred, get your butt down here right away. Your mama is fixin' to kill Carol."

"What do you mean?"

She explained that Carol was in intensive care, and the day before, her physician called our mother to tell her that Carol might not make it through the night.

"Your mother suggested they take her off life support—over the phone! What kind of mother does that? Your mother and Ann are flying down tomorrow. I need somebody to keep an eye on them when I'm at work, so they don't stand on her oxygen tube."

I arrived in Dallas later that day, rented a car, and drove directly to the hospital in Plano, where Pam met me after her meeting with the lawyer. According to Texas law at the time, she needed a medical power of attorney, as well as her regular power of attorney. Foremost in her mind were the protracted legal battles that surrounded Karen Ann Quinlan, who had lain in a persistent vegetative state for ten years. Pam felt better once she signed the papers. And when Ann and my mother arrived later, we began to see that they posed no real threat. They were as scared as we were. My mother, at eighty, had grown frail and diminutive.

Ann looked drawn and worn out. There was a gray pallor to her face that showed signs of the on-going dissolution of her marriage and her first cancer scare, neither of which she spoke about. The doctors assured us that my mother did not have the authority to make medical decisions, nor could she override the do not resuscitate order that Carol had signed some years earlier. What struck me is how much power we assumed my mother had, and how much fear we had all been living in.

In the days that followed, Carol hovered between this world and the next. A kind of netherworld, or so I imagined, populated by voices without bodies, images moving in and out of focus, a floating world, a state of semiconsciousness, yet not quite a dream. A place of waiting, which I'd come to know in my own way over the past twelve years, my ear tuned to the telephone, more bad news, the final bad news: Come. She's dying. For real this time.

At the funeral parlor, my mother and Ann stood off by themselves, between the rubber tree and a high-backed red plush chair, so my mother could sit down if her feet got tired. The receiving line didn't seem to be working quite the way it did in St. Louis. Two of the women from the pathology lab went over to give their condolences, then realized they had nothing much to say, having never actually met Carol.

"I bet it's hotter here in Dallas than it is up in St. Louis," said one. "It's hot even for Texas this early in the year."

"I was in St. Louis once," said the other. "Such a lovely city. So many trees. What's the name of that big park you have?"

"Forest Park," said my mother.

"Yes, that's it. So lovely. Anyway, we are so very sorry for your loss, Mrs. Adler."

"DePew," said my mother. "Adler was my daughter's married name."

"Of course," said the woman. "Well, anyway, we're sorry."

The women drifted back to the slide show.

Meanwhile, the lesbians were working it out in their minds how to approach my mother and sister—what to say when asked how they knew Carol.

"Carol and Pam used to come watch us play softball," one said, giving Ann's hand a vigorous shake. "They were some of our biggest fans."

"They were even bigger fans of the Dallas Cowboys," said another. "Carol sure did love football."

"Ever since she was little," said Ann. "She was a water boy for the high-school team."

"I saw that in the slide show," said the first woman. "We're sure going to miss her."

"I know," said Ann. "So will we."

Three months earlier, Pam called to tell me that Carol'd had a setback and the hospital had sent her home with oxygen. No one could say with any confidence what the prognosis was. Whether or not this was "it," Pam wanted me there.

I flew to Dallas, rented a car, and, as always, followed Pam's simple directions to their house via the North Central Expressway onto West Spring Creek Parkway, right on Custer, then right onto Cumberland, just before the Custer Road United Methodist Church, which was enormous. I always said a little prayer of thanksgiving to them for creating a landmark I could see from far enough away that I had time to get into the right-hand turn lane.

The house was closed and dark, as usual. All the blinds were pulled against the sun—even in February. A blue haze of cigarette smoke hung in all the rooms. The only actual fresh air that got into the house came when Pam slid the glass door in the kitchen open to let the dogs in or out or when she opened the front door to get the mail.

Pam had set herself up in the den in front of the TV set. I was to sleep in the guest room, which they called Pam's room when my mother visited. Carol was in their bedroom at the back. The whole house felt like a sickroom—stagnant, tense, everything clenched against pain. I went to sit with Carol, who was in and out of consciousness. Mostly she slept, a fitful, shallow sleep, waking up with a start from time to time—terrified, gasping for breath.

She knew I was there. She said she was glad I had come. And then she drifted off again. I just sat with her. There was nothing I could do to make her more comfortable, so I closed my eyes and breathed the stale air. I didn't know what to pray for. Her recovery and improved health? Or a swift release from the pain she had suffered for the past twelve years, and, in a sense, most of her life. I settled on: God help me to be in this love.

As I sat at the foot of what might have been her deathbed, we both drifted in and out of . . . something—the present, the past, floating in the space between worlds. At one point, she thought I was a favorite cousin, with whom she'd spent summers in Maine at a cottage our grandparents rented each year, so I sat in for him and held that memory with her until we were both set adrift again in our separate streams.

"Can you light me a cigarette?" she asked in a raspy voice.

"Carol," I said, "you're on oxygen. You'll blow the place up!"

"Oh no, no, no," she wheezed. "They've improved them. You can smoke now. The doctor said it was okay."

I reluctantly lit a cigarette and handed it to her. She drew from it a few times, then leaned over and dropped it on the rug as she tried to reach the ashtray on her bedside table. I swooped down to pick it up.

"Okay," I said. "Here's the new rule. No smoking unless somebody else is in the room with you." I put her pack of cigarettes and lighter in a drawer in the dresser across the room, knowing full well she couldn't get out of bed on her own to fetch them.

On the day before I was to go back home, I sat with Carol as she slept. She woke up and said, "I keep trying to figure out what I did to deserve this."

"Nothing," I said. "You did nothing to bring this on yourself. You are not to blame for being ill."

And yet I recognized the belief, that somehow illness is a judgment from God, a punishment handed down through the Old Testament, the New Testament, the Catholic Church, the harsh and unforgiving Protestant theologies. It was even subtly and insidiously embedded in New Age theories. It was somehow our own fault. Eve ate the apple. We smoked. We drank. We worked at the paper mill. We lived too close to the nuclear waste dump. We didn't have enough faith, or the right kind of faith. We never dealt properly with our childhood trauma. From the book of Job right down through Louise Hay, we only had ourselves to blame.

Even so, when I told Carol that her illness was not her fault, I meant it. I knew it was true. Not only had she done nothing wrong to bring on her illness, it was nobody else's fault either. Recovery from alcoholism had freed us once and for all from a social system based on fear, shame, inadequacy, and keeping up appearances. It wasn't a matter of what caused our ills as much as it was the healing path we chose. And once we had surrendered to love, blame ceased to be an issue.

Rowlett Creek Cemetery was about a ten-minute drive from the funeral parlor. Pam had hired a stretch limousine for the four of us. Others followed in their own cars. The hearse drove through the raised single-bar gate of the graveyard. The rest of us parked outside and made our way through the phlox, thistle, and buttercup blooming between the headstones. The lesbians got to the chairs that had been set up underneath a sycamore tree and were careful to fill the back rows, while Pam and I helped my mother and Ann down the hill, which was slow going because their high heels kept sinking into the mud.

The plot Carol had chosen was up a slight incline from where Pam would be buried. "She wanted to make sure her spot didn't get flooded in a hard rain. This way, I get the downflow," Pam said. She didn't see that it mattered since they'd both be dead. What mattered is they'd still be together. On one of my earlier visits to Plano, Carol had shown me where she wanted to be buried. The cemetery was maybe the last acreage anywhere around that still felt rural. The graves were mostly old. Little Confederate flags fluttered in the breeze above some of them, and long grass grew in the open areas. Plano's current prosperous residents preferred the newer upscale cemeteries.

Carol had stood under one of the large shade trees and pointed toward a meadow spread with yellow wildflowers.

"I like the view," she said.

"It won't be there when it comes time to bury us," said Pam. "It'll be sold for houses."

"It'll be there," said Carol, without explaining further. She meant the land itself, the stones, the snakes, the prairie grasses that would go on growing uninterrupted by yet another subdivision. "It'll be there," she said, her eyes fixed on a point in the distance.

"What if Mom wants you buried in St. Louis?" I asked.

"You can't let her do it," she said. "This is where I lived my life."

"Dearly beloved, we are gathered here today to remember Carol De-Pew Adler, who left us too soon." Reverend Bob read from a black binder that looked like it might hold a diploma. "Today we celebrate the life of someone who"—he glanced at his notes—"loved animals and had a wonderful sense of humor. She was raised in St. Louis, where she graduated from John Burroughs School and later attended Centenary College in Massachusetts."

"Connecticut," Pam interrupted.

"New Jersey," my mother corrected her.

Reverend Bob took a deep breath and continued. "And Baylor Nursing School right here in Dallas." He looked at Pam. She nodded. He glanced at my mother. She smiled. "She was good at tennis and played in some tournaments when she was young. She also excelled at field hockey and girls' basketball in high school. People here in Dallas remember her as a loyal friend, a good listener, someone you could confide in, but also someone who was full of fun and loved steak and mashed potatoes. She will be sorely missed by her mother, Mrs. C. D. DePew Jr.; her sister, Ann; her brother Alfred; and her dear friend Pam."

Brief and to the point, if the point was to keep a foolish and childish old woman from knowing what really mattered to her daughter—the last twenty-five years with her lover, the courage, the leap of faith it had required to make herself vulnerable enough to be loved. For their first ten years together, Carol kept an overnight bag packed and ready by the front door, just in case things didn't work out.

Pam turned to a large boom box resting on a nearby headstone and pushed the button. Barbra Streisand's voice sang the Lord's Prayer from her best-selling Christmas album, one of Carol's favorites.

Then it was time to go. The gravediggers stood next to the backhoe, waiting to do their job once we left. One of the lesbians came up to offer her condolences. I thanked her and asked if she was coming back to Pam's house.

"No," she said. "I'm playing in a football game this afternoon."

"Well then," I said, "hit 'em hard—for Carol."

"You bet," she said, grinning, and gave me a wink.

Once back at Pam's house, we sat and stood around eating chicken sandwiches cut into triangles, macaroni salad, chips with guacamole, and an assortment of cookies.

"Carol sure liked Coca-Cola," someone said.

"She got that from her mama," said Pam. "Isn't that right, Mrs. DePew?"

"She most certainly did," replied my mother. "She most certainly did."

A year later, I returned to Plano to mark the first anniversary of Carol's passing. Pam and I sat at her kitchen table drinking a fresh pot of coffee. She lit a cigarette.

"My mama grew up in the Great Depression. They lived outside of town, not far from the railroad tracks. Hobos would stop at the kitchen door from time to time. Not one of them went away empty-handed, even if it was only a potato or a crust of bread. That's just how people did back then. Carol was like that, you know. She'd give you the shirt off her back. She had so much love in her."

"She kept bringing home stray dogs," I said. "Sometimes she'd carry them into the backyard and claim they followed her."

"Then there was that time she traded you for a pony."

I rolled my eyes and shook my head.

"She was nobody's fool," said Pam. "She knew a good deal when she saw one."

"That she did."

Pam poured herself more coffee.

"I tried to get the hearse, but they wouldn't rent it to me without a casket to put in it. I wanted us to follow it in the stretch limousine from the funeral home to the cemetery again."

I opened my mouth to say something, but thought better of it.

"Camie talked me out of the limousine. She said it didn't make sense to spend all that money, but I wanted it to be just like it was last year. I was so busy taking care of everybody, I felt like I missed the whole thing, like it never even happened. Camie's going to set it all up like it was. She told everybody when to arrive, and all we have to do is drive there. She's even arranged for lunch to be here when we come back."

The next day, I offered to drive to the cemetery, but Pam said, "The way you get lost around here, I best drive. It'll be quicker, and we won't have to get into a fight."

Camie and some of the other women had set up chairs in a semicircle. There weren't going to be that many of us. She'd put the boom box on a nearby headstone. Once Pam sat down, we gathered around her, and she started telling stories about Carol: the fateful 1980 Super Bowl game ("I was sure the Rams were going to win that game, but

Carol bet me a steak dinner that it would be the Steelers. And sure enough, the Steelers took it"), Carol moving in and getting sober.

"There was this one time. Carol had stopped drinking, but she fell off the wagon. We had a terrible fight and she stormed out of the house. I was afraid I'd seen the last of her, but later that night, she appeared at the front door, her shoes covered in mud, with a bunch of plastic yellow roses in her hand. 'Here,' she said. 'They're for you. I'm sorry.' Turns out she'd stolen them from this very cemetery. Driven around the gate over somebody's gravestone, scraped the hell out of the bottom of her car. She said she used to come here to think. She's got all the time in the world for that now."

One story followed another, and each story came alive in loving detail.

"There was this other time, in Oklahoma. Up at Lake Murray. We loved going there and went as often as Carol was well enough to make the drive. It was raining one day when we were there, and she said let's go to the chapel, so we did. We went in and sat still, listening to the rain on the roof, just the two of us. It was so peaceful. Then she took my hand and said, 'I promise to go on loving you more than I've ever loved anyone else, and I promise to try to be good to you and deserve your love—for as long as we both shall live. What do you promise?' I said I promised to keep taking out the garbage and taking the dogs to the vet and paying the mortgage. And she said, 'I'm serious. What do you promise?'"

Pam stopped to light a cigarette and looked out over the gravestones, her forearms on her knees. "I said, 'You're the best thing that ever happened to me. My life wouldn't have meant anything without you. I promise to keep loving you and caring for you and laughing at your jokes.'" Pam turned and looked at each one of us and said, "We had twenty-five years together. She was my mate. That's the way it was. And nobody can change that or take it away from me."

After a moment, she leaned over, pushed the Play button on the boom box, and we listened to Barbra Streisand sing the Lord's Prayer.

Palm Springs: Bonfire of the Banalities

From the darkened bedroom where I lie as still as possible, I hear someone shout "No" from the living room and fear that the toilets have backed up into the shower drains again, but since I am trying to avoid any sudden movement or unnecessary excitement, I stay where I am with my eyes closed, waiting for this headache to go away.

Yesterday, my first full day in Palm Springs, I managed to get too much sun, though I anointed myself with liberal amounts of strong lotion and sat mostly under the umbrella and came back inside regularly to fetch more water. But the sun here has a liquid quality and seeps under any kind of shade, as if it were humidity.

This is the California desert. In August. When no one in his right mind would choose to be here.

Except that friends from Paris have rented a house, and I cannot yet imagine visiting France because it has been thirty-five years since I was there to renew my English visa—when the theater company I worked for in London was falling apart, and the relationship I was in was falling apart—and I'm more than a little afraid of the memories I am likely to encounter.

I don't want to think about that, so I lie as still as I can and listen to the roar of the air conditioner as it blows so much cold air down over me that I have to get under the quilt. I want to think about when the sun goes down, and it is safe to sit outside and look at the moon and shooting stars. I want to think of the extraordinary mountain we face when we sit by the pool in back of the house.

When I do venture outdoors in daylight, I cannot stop looking at this mountain. Brown and rocky, it rises from the flat valley like the shoulder of someone turning away in sleep. I lose track of the conversation around the pool, a list of movie stars and indiscretions, gossip that is sixty or seventy years old.

People say Palm Springs is Disneyland for adults, a perpetual cocktail party, a Hollywood invention of the 1940s and '50s, frozen in time or dried like dead flowers. Others call it God's waiting room for the preponderance of retirees. I'm told that half the town is gay and votes "blue" for the Democrats and the other half are right-wing fundamentalists who vote "red," which now refers to Republicans and not Communists.

A significant change from the 1950s.

On the way to dinner, one of the Parisians asks for a definition of American kitsch, and someone mentions Liberace, who owned a number of houses in Palm Springs.

"No," I say with surprising authority. "That's high camp."

The novelist Milan Kundera defines kitsch as an aesthetic "in which shit is denied and everyone acts as though it did not exist." And I think about what the plumbers have been cleaning out of the shower drains in the house where we are staying. "Kitsch," says Kundera, "excludes everything from its purview which is essentially unacceptable in human existence."

Like death.

We're on our way to Monday-night Sissy Bingo at the Ace Hotel led by a six foot eight drag queen named Bella da Ball and her tiny sidekick, retired New York City singer Linda Gerard, who has us guessing the titles of Noël Coward and Cole Porter songs by first singing their long intros. Bella welcomes everybody as they come in, asks where they're from. Germany. France. Austin, Texas. I am one of three Canadians in the crowd. Bella wears a lime green wig that adds another foot to his height, a bright flowered miniskirt, and a sweater because the air conditioner is on too high. Later in the show, he explains that he's been calling bingo since he was a little boy in Minnesota church basements.

The bingo is fun. The food is good. The drag queen is nice, not bitchy. I wouldn't expect anything else from a Minnesotan. And there are prizes, a lot of laughing, and some pretty good songs.

The singer explains that she is just back from three months off being sick, and as we leave, I stop to thank her. She tells me she has stage four cancer and is singing with only one lung.

"Can you tell?" she asks, looking worried.

"No," I say.

"I don't know where you were pulling that voice from," says my friend. "Your heart, I guess."

"Or my ass!" She laughs and then starts coughing.

What strikes me about Palm Springs is what strikes me about any desert I have visited. A vast sense of geological time. When this was the bottom of an inland sea. The relentless white light of the sun. The unlikelihood of survival. Scorpions. Rattlesnakes. Vultures circling overhead.

Waiting.

Don't Shoot, I'm Canadian

In March 2013, Kris Kleindienst and her then-husband and co-owner of Left Bank Books decided to publish my second collection of stories. I was on my way back home to western Canada from Maine, and we were having breakfast at a South St. Louis diner. I'm not sure how the subject came up. I was most likely grousing about my lack of success placing the collection, which had been rejected by all twelve of the small presses I most admired in Canada, as well as any number of publishers in the United States.

"Why don't we publish it?" Kris said.

"Sure. Why not?" said Jay.

"We've been talking about starting a small press through the bookstore for some time now."

"What shall we call it?" Jay asked.

"How about Mixed Messages Press?" Kris laughed.

Jay searched the name on his phone. The web address was available. We looked at one another, stunned, but not for long. What followed was a rapid-fire exchange of ideas, things to consider, details to be worked out along the way. We were well fed, highly caffeinated, and giddy with possibilities.

On August 9, 2014, the Ferguson, Missouri, police officer Darren Wilson shot and killed a Black teenager, Michael Brown, and left his body unattended in the street for four hours. Canadians looked on in horror as things went from bad to worse with the slow contorted logic of a nightmare. The violence came in waves. We were inundated with images of police firing tear gas canisters and rubber bullets into crowds of protesters, burning buildings, overturned cars, and contradictory information—there were or weren't witnesses, Brown was shot in the police cruiser, he was shot outside the car; the officer was or was not provoked, did or did not act in self-defense. The Missouri State Highway Patrol intervened, "relieving Ferguson and St. Louis County officers of their law enforcement authority" as the Associated Press put it. The FBI opened an investigation.

Kris and Jay were pitched headlong into community action at the bookstore, as well as panic about how to keep their son, a dark-skinned Hispanic high schooler, out of harm's way. News of Brown's death hit me hard. How was this even happening in 2014, with Barack Obama in the White House? I left St. Louis in 1975. I lived in France, Spain, and England, settling in Maine in 1981. In 2012, I became a Canadian citizen. And yet the news touched every fiber of my being: outrage, disbelief, grief—and underneath it all, a sickening shame. Something about the killing of Michael Brown was not surprising at all.

I was in the grip of something old. Familiar. Familial. I am descended from abolitionists. Everyone on both sides of the family fought with the Union Army. Even the Quakers broke ranks with the Society of Friends and went to war. Or so the story goes. And yet their descendants, my parents and grandparents, saw nothing wrong with racial segregation and the Jim Crow laws that held it in place. They viewed the freedom fighters registering Black voters in the South with contempt and derision, which was complicated—skewed and exacerbated—by chronic alcoholism.

I grew up in an all-white suburb, went to all-white schools, which, however well-meaning and progressive they were in their methods, prepared us to be privileged, superior, and white. The only Black people we saw tended the grounds, mopped the floors, and prepared our food. True, many of our teachers had Black friends and colleagues and neighbors, but our teachers themselves, though worthy of our respect, were our social inferiors. It was a world full of distinctions, demarcations, and boundaries you only found out about when you crossed them. The Saturday-evening dance lessons in the basement of the Congregational Church gave way to dances at the St. Louis Country Club, and the Jewish kids disappeared. No one could explain why. They had their own country club, we were told.

But it was also the 1960s and the social fabric was coming unraveled—fast. With the help and full support of many of our teachers, we were calling for change, insisting that we apply what we were learning—both in and out of the classroom—about justice, fairness, and redressing wrongs. We set up tutoring programs at settlement houses, organized workshops, held symposia. We wrote articles and editorials in the school newspaper, worked on political campaigns, helped staff the draft counseling centers, wore black armbands, handed out leaflets, attended lectures, joined marches. I hesitate to ridicule the teenager I was in those days, struggling to do the right thing, though I was driven by white liberal guilt and inflated by self-righteous moral indignation. I do not want to minimize the courage it took for me to register for the draft as a conscientious objector without the support of my family or a community of faith. But I also want to acknowledge the fact that I had what many Black eighteen-year-olds did not have—a student deferment. With all my awareness and goodwill, it was my white privilege that too often made the difference.

In his book, *My Grandmother's Hands,* the American psychologist Resmaa Menakem points out that everything white people have done to Black people in the United States, white people did to each other in Europe—in the years of religious wars, witch burnings, hangings (lynchings), and scapegoating each other during plagues. The history of racism is also the history of undigested trauma. Menakem goes on to say that racialized trauma lives in our bodies, whether we are white or Black. And it's not only the trauma we ourselves have experienced. We carry the "unhealed dissonance and trauma of our ancestors." As valuable as cognitive therapies are, until we metabolize our own trauma and that of our ancestors, very little, if anything, changes, and we end up perpetuating systemic racism, despite our best intentions not to.

My own twelve-step recovery educated me about family systems, and I started tracing generational patterns of drinking and what seemed like alcoholic behavior in my ancestors who were known to be strict teetotalers. What I found were lapses of memory, an absence of stories of any kind, secrets, childhood sexual abuse, shame—a legacy of unhealed suffering. My first job, of course, was to attend to my own recovery, but I also began to notice shifts in my family, especially in two of my siblings who were also in recovery, but also in my mother who was not. What's more, I sensed movement, a kind of release, in and around my father, whose death had nudged me into recovery in the first place.

On November 22, I arrived in St. Louis for the book launch. Five days earlier, Missouri's governor declared a state of emergency and called out the National Guard, setting the stage for whatever would unfold in anticipation of the grand jury's decision. I picked up my rental car and headed to my cousin Steve's house, where I'd be staying for the next ten days. Steve was five years older and went to a different school, so we never got to know each other growing up. I knew his younger brother and sister better. Steve and I had grown close after he married Jody, whom he met while teaching high school in Maine, where I now lived. In time, they started coming to Maine each summer, and I would drive up to their lakeside camp for a lobster bake and to spend the night. Steve had been very close to my sister Carol, so we had her in common, but we also shared a love of teaching. He was currently practicing law in St. Louis. I had often wondered how Jody was adapting to the suburbs, having been raised in a farming community outside Augusta, Maine. When I saw her in the summer, she looked relieved to be home.

The morning after I arrived, Jody and I sat over coffee in the kitchen. I asked her how she was dealing with the events in and around Ferguson at the progressive, independent elementary school where she taught science.

"We don't talk about it," she said.

"But how is that even possible?"

"It's too upsetting for the children."

"What's the conversation in the teachers' lounge, then?"

"There isn't one," she said. "When someone brought it up early in the school year, a teacher ran from the room, crying."

We both knew how crazy that was—not only as educators but also in terms of functional human behavior. What I was quick to discover is that few people actually had access to the frontal lobe of their brain. The whole community was in some form of trauma, no matter what a person's political leanings were. Their world had become a madhouse—irrational, violent, and fear-driven. Jody didn't like what was happening at her school, but the heaviness in the air, something akin to the collective shadow, rendered her powerless. She too was silenced by the group mind, "for the sake of the children," who we both knew were being harmed more by silence than by the pain of truthful dialogue.

And yet I knew something about the cost of breaking that silence. I published my first book of stories in 1992. When I arrived in St. Louis for a reading at Left Bank, my mother opened her front door, said hello with a kiss and a hug, and then said, "Your aunt Hope is very upset by your book. She said you're not to call her." In that short exchange with my mother I was confronted with much of what I'd had to overcome to write in the first place, never mind finding the courage to publish. In one of the stories, based on memories of my grandmother's sister, I had revealed a secret that I was to find out was the source of my grandmother's deepest shame, a shame that I now see had impinged upon my father's life and most likely was a contributing factor in his own crippling silences and chronic depression. I had inadvertently lanced a primary wound in the family, and I had to pay the price. Betrayal had consequences.

The grand jury was scheduled to announce their decision on a Monday evening. That morning, I was to have breakfast with my eldest sister's partner, a man I didn't much like, but who had shown deep love and compassion for Ann in the last years of her life. By 2014, he had developed dementia and was in an assisted-living facility in Clayton. When I picked him up, I helped him to review the list of what he needed to remember that day and made sure he had the keys to his apartment. I was driving. He was the navigator.

"Turn left here," said Robb. "It's on Forsyth."

We drove along Forsyth, but didn't find the restaurant.

"What's it called?" I asked.

"I don't remember," he said. "I'll know when I see it. Maybe it's on Maryland."

We tried Maryland. No luck. Turns out it was on Ladue Road, and when we pulled into the strip mall, we saw that it was closed. In fact most of the neighborhood storefronts were boarded up against the violence they anticipated that evening. I drove up one street and down another until we found a diner open across from the county courthouse, which would later be surrounded by the National Guard.

Two men sat at the counter. All of the tables were empty. Robb and I sat down at one of them. We were the only white people. Robb made a snide comment, I forget what now, but it was beyond inappropriate; it was hostile. His jokes always had been. Even before his dementia, he'd been tactless. I suspect he imagined it was part of his naughty-boy charm, but I found it offensive. I was here out of some form of loyalty to my sister who had died of cancer three years earlier. For all his faults, Robb had seen her through round after round of chemotherapy and radiation and had invited her to move in with him after our mother died. An unrepentant racist, he had shown an unfailing patience, compassion, and deep love for my sister, who, because of him, had died at home in the presence of her daughter and my cousin Steve who had just happened to stop by to say hello.

The waitress came over to take our order. I smiled and asked how her day was going. She just looked at me.

"Well," I said. "I'll have two eggs over easy, crisp bacon, and buttered toast, please. What'll you have, Robb?" He gave me a blank look. "For breakfast. What would you like to eat for breakfast?" I pointed to the menu in his hands. "Give us a minute," I said to the waitress.

It was as if he had forgotten what breakfast was and was listening, his head cocked, to the sound of the word—the same two notes on a piano: DAdum, DAdum.

"Breakfast," I repeated. "Would you like eggs? Bacon? How about some cereal? Oh look! They have cinnamon rolls!"

His face seemed to brighten, so I walked up to the counter to compete our order.

"And some coffee when you get a moment. Thanks, so much."

The men at the counter gave me a sidelong glance.

When our breakfasts came, she put the cinnamon roll in front of Robb, who looked up and said, "I want eggs!"

I turned to our server and said, "It's okay. I'll handle this."

I switched our plates, smiling hard.

"I don't like runny yokes," he cried. "I want scrambled!"

Doing my best to hide the rage that had lodged in my throat, I said as clearly and calmly as I could, "Eat the toast and bacon. We have to leave, Robb. They're about to close."

"But why are they closing?"

I stood up and pulled on my jacket. "Come on. Make sure you have everything. We need to leave. Now. Not another word until we're in the car."

All I knew was that I had to get Robb back to his apartment. I placed a twenty on the counter with our check and said, "Keep the change. And thank you so much for your patience." I wanted to say, Forgive me. My friend has dementia; it's not his fault. I wanted to say, Look, I'm on your side. I'm Canadian. This has nothing to do with me.

But we both knew there was no excuse. For any of it.

That evening, I sat with friends from high school in a Webster Groves restaurant, staring up at a TV screen with everyone else, including servers and bartenders, waiting for the grand jury's announcement. Their decision: not to prosecute the police officer. Our response: a silence that was hard to read. Stunned, but also wary, cautious. No one dared even an audible intake of breath, much less a cry of "Foul!," "No!," or "Good! The cop was innocent!" I was trying hard not to have an opinion. But my Canadian citizenship had not earned me the right of an innocent bystander. If I remember correctly, everyone in the restaurant was white—at least everyone I could see. I don't know about the kitchen staff. We settled our bill and got ready to leave as the screen showed one group of protesters beginning to respond in Ferguson and another group marching north on Grand Boulevard to block Highway 40, the main artery connecting downtown St. Louis to the western suburbs, the symbolic and literal route of white flight in the 1950s and '60s. Ron and Janey and I decided it was best for me to go directly to my cousin's house, though my normal route didn't involve Highway 40, and I shouldn't have any trouble getting there. But anything could happen, and it was best to be cautious. I was coming to their house for dinner the following Saturday, so we could talk more then. Getting into my car I realized that I had grown unused to this kind of fear, but my body remembered. It was a fear that was subtly but consistently drilled into me, a fear of all things east of Skinker Boulevard—working-class neighborhoods, some integrated, some segregated, large houses on private streets under siege from Black thieves and rapists, Black ghettos, housing projects. My body remembered a time in Paris when I had almost gotten caught in a mass demonstration that police were about to break up with bludgeons and tear gas. And I had lived in Spain the year after Franco's death, when it was still under the rule of Fascists and military police.

Back at my cousin's house, I found everyone in front of the large flat-screen TV mounted on the wall of their family room, watching in silence. On one side of the split screen, President Obama called for calm and faith in the due process of law. The other side showed people chanting, shouting, and overturning cars against a backdrop of burning buildings in Ferguson. The image of the president dissolved into aerial images of people swarming onto Highway 40 to block traffic.

Steve turned to me and said he'd been to the gun shop earlier in the day to pick up one of his duck-hunting rifles, which they'd repaired.

"The place was full of people buying these handguns that fire buckshot. They call them 'the Judge,'" he said. "And the owner said these guys were buying them like crazy." He shook his head.

"I'm not scared," said my cousin's teenaged daughter. "The Ladue Police Station is just up the road, less than a mile away." She aimed the remote control at the screen and pressed a button to return to what they'd been watching before the news bulletin, an episode of *The Hunger Games,* which showed crowds of people storming what looked like a castle.

Once the others had gone to bed, I asked Steve what he thought of the situation—as a lawyer. He explained that the grand jury's function was not to determine guilt or innocence, but to decide whether or not there was sufficient evidence to justify proceeding with charges against the police officer. In this case, there was a lack of eyewitnesses, the events in the convenience store immediately preceding Brown's encounter with the police, and whether or not Brown's behavior constituted a threat to the police officer's life. My cousin's area of expertise was corporate and not criminal law, but those were his thoughts. I wondered about his more personal thoughts, but it was late. I was emotionally wrung out, and we'd have other opportunities to talk. Or so I hoped.

The next morning, Annie, the Black woman who worked for Steve's family, and I had the kitchen to ourselves, so I asked what she thought about what was happening.

"All I know," she said, "is that poor white boy was scared out of his mind." I realized that not once in the last three months had I considered what it might have felt like to be twenty-eight-year-old police officer Darren Wilson that day, what went through his mind and body, what may or may not have contributed to his pulling the trigger twelve times. Regardless of how scared Wilson may have been, as Menakem points out, when a police officer "unnecessarily harms" a Black person, "all attention is typically deflected away from police culture—and from a widespread pattern of behavior—and onto a particular officer and the particular incident under scrutiny. The incident is treated by police culture as an anomaly, when—as in Ferguson, Missouri—the widespread pattern is painfully evident. . . Ultimately, as part of that same pattern, the officer is often not held accountable because, as they tell the investigator or the grand jury, 'I feared for my life,' or 'I was scared to death' . . ."

"We need to take these phrases very seriously," says Menakem. "In some instances, they are not a dodge but an honest description of the trauma-inspired fight, flee, or freeze … response. The lizard brain has sensed a threat, overridden the thinking brain, and sent out an order to destroy. When seen this way, many apparently senseless murders become more understandable. This does not, however, make lizard-brain panic a valid defense for murder."

On Saturday night, I went to Ron and Janey's house for dinner. Other guests included Ron's nephew, wife, and little boy, as well as one of the nephew's colleagues from Fox News, who was in town from New York to cover the Ferguson protests. Ron introduced me as his old high-school friend who now lived in Canada and wrote a column for an online newspaper, which of course was not a newspaper, but I couldn't get used to saying I wrote for a website, and I refused to call it a blog, though of course that is what it was.

"He's in town promoting his new book," said Janey.

"Oh," said Ron's nephew, "what's it about?"

I said it was a collection of fiction, stories, and two novellas, one set in Santa Fe about a painter and tensions that arise between him and his patron, who has a new boyfriend, and the other about a theater company's production of Bertolt Brecht's *Threepenny Opera* that goes wrong in Leningrad in the summer of 1993. His eyes glazed over; his smile remained fixed. Given everything that was going on, the book seemed ridiculous, irreverent, and even somehow offensive.

The talk turned to covering the news, the use of flak jackets and other protective gear, as if they were covering a war, which in a sense they were, a war whose origins no one seemed able or willing to name. Nothing that the young man from Fox News said sounded anything like journalism. I wondered who was covering the story here on the ground. Who had been listening to people in the community for more than the ten minutes it took to grab a sound bite? Where had these reporters been since August? Someone, somewhere had to be addressing the questions of chronic unemployment, the wildly disproportionate number of Black men in prisons, and the privatization of those prisons for profit, not to mention the militarization of the police. Sure, there were the late-night talk-show hosts and comedians and the very courageous Rachel Maddow, but something was missing.

I wanted to tell them a story I'd heard from another St. Louis friend about members of her synagogue joining forces with Baptists, Buddhists, Catholics, Quakers, and others who were inserting themselves between the protesters and the police to remind people on both sides to keep looking at each other. Why was no one telling that story? I glanced at Ron, a lifelong left-leaning liberal, well informed and with strong opinions. I saw that he was intent on keeping the peace, so I took my cue and held my tongue. But I was more and more troubled by the silence, the terrible absence of any real dialogue. I remembered endless, heated discussions throughout the turbulent, crisis-ridden 1960s, when no matter how angry we were at one another, we still talked. Until, I guess, we didn't.

The next morning, I went with Steve and his family to the church I had attended as a teenager. I'd forgotten how beautiful it was—pale blue walls, white trim, simple brass chandeliers, light streaming in through the clear glass in tall windows. No statues. No bric-a-brac. What people call low-church Episcopalian. My eldest sister had married the minister's son in 1963, and I was confirmed five years later.

In April 1968, I had just turned sixteen and was a new driver. My first time driving to church on my own, I was about to make a left turn when the light changed from green to yellow, and I slammed on the brakes. The pickup truck behind me ran into the back of my car. We weren't going fast enough to do any real damage, but of course I was shaken, even more so when I got out of the car and saw that the driver of the truck was a Black man, who was every bit as shaken, if not more so, than I was. Dr. Martin Luther King Jr. had been assassinated three days earlier, we were in an all-white suburb, and in every city in the United States, people were in the streets, giving voice to their outrage and grief.

We stood by the side of the road and exchanged phone and license plate numbers. I now realize that the fear in my body included a generalized fear of Black men that white children learned by osmosis in a white supremacist culture, even when my body also knew there were Black men in my life whom I trusted implicitly. There was another facet to this fear, informed by the fear I sensed in his body. At sixteen, I knew that this man's life was in danger and that the danger had something to do with me and the fact that I was white. We both knew that he needed to get on with his business and out of that neighborhood as fast as possible. I went ahead to church, slipped into a back pew, and knelt in prayer, trying to hide my shaking hands and irregular breathing.

I don't recall anything about the sermon that day, but I doubt it addressed what was on my heart. In the months and years that followed I grew increasingly troubled by the lack of response by that particular parish to other churches' calls for social justice, and began to wonder at what point Christian diplomacy actually began to collude with evil.

This Sunday, forty-six years later, I sat next to my cousin six days after the grand jury's decision not to prosecute a white cop in the shooting death of a Black teenager. And in one of those weird twists of destiny, another, though more distant, relative now climbed into the pulpit to give the sermon. He addressed the events in Ferguson directly, citing Dr. King's 1963 "Letter from Birmingham Jail," his answer to eight white religious leaders in the South who had written to King urging restraint. "Justice too long delayed is justice denied." I did nothing to hide the tears streaming down my face. This was the sermon I needed to hear when I was sixteen. As I listened, I felt something shift in me, and for the first time since my plane had landed eight days earlier, I could take a full breath. On my way out, I thanked the priest for his courage and left it at that.

The following Tuesday evening was the book launch. I arrived two hours early to sign copies for the store and so that Jay could make a short promotional video to post on social media. The National Guard had been called off, but things were still tense. We were all exhausted. It was the week after Thanksgiving and the bookstore was gearing up for the Christmas rush. Their social justice work and community organizing continued unabated. I was running on fumes, focused on the last bit of distance to the finish line and my flight home the next day. Jay set me up at a table in the basement with a pile of books and a pen. My mood lightened, and I began to look forward to the evening. I was among long-time friends and fellow travelers, continuing the publishing adventure we'd begun twenty months earlier.

I chose a scene from the Santa Fe novella to read that evening—something light and funny. But as I began I felt the room go flat, and each time I looked up to connect with my listeners, I was met with twenty or so blank smiling faces, as if they were waiting for me to begin, as if the microphone had been off and they hadn't heard a word, as if I'd been reading in another language and they were waiting hopefully for a simultaneous translation. When it was clear to them that I had stopped, they were good enough to clap.

Then Kris and I sat on high stools and began what was probably the most awkward and emotionally fraught conversation of our forty-year friendship. We did our best, but there was so much weighing on us. Days—for Kris, weeks, months—of hypervigilance, interior red alert. One ear tuned to the street. If protesters and police started swarming outside the window, did we duck and cover, or stand and wave the Old Red Flag? I had read at Left Bank any number of times since my first book came out in 1992, but I'd never felt this strange. I hoped that neither of us looked as distraught as we felt. Soon enough, and mercifully, it was over. People were gracious. They bought books. I signed them. In years past, we had gone out for a drink or something to eat afterward, or we had stood around in the bookstore, savoring the celebration, but we'd all been squeezed dry. There was nothing more to say, for the moment. We gathered our things, hugged, and agreed to touch base after Christmas. I drove to my cousin's house to pack and get some sleep.

As I joined the line to board my plane to Toronto the next afternoon, I noticed the man in front of me staring up at a TV screen. I followed his glance to an image of a white policeman kneeling on the neck of a Black man, who was struggling to say, "I can't breathe." In the next moment, Eric Garner was dead. Right there on the screen. How was that possible? But there it was again, the same sequence. And again—over and over—an instant replay, as a voice-over examined in close detail the officer's technique. Over and over to imprint the new rule of law: a death penalty without benefit of a trial. Which of course was not at all new for Black people, especially Black men. By the time I handed my boarding pass to the agent, my carefully cultivated detachment had vanished, and I was in the grip of the kind of tribal rage that could only seek revenge. The lizard brain had me at last.

Once back home in Vancouver, I got to work sending out books and publicity packets to Canadian reviewers and organizing a local launch at the public library. Meanwhile, it took me a long time to sort out what had happened. I thought of devoting some of my *Vancouver Observer* columns to it, incorporating interviews I had conducted with various Black St. Louisans, including a policewoman. But I lost my nerve, lost heart. Too much stood in the way—inside and outside. Waves of grief and shame and rage prevented me from writing anything at all about it. I continued to look with a deepening sense of hopelessness as things in the States went from bad to worse—again and again and again.

A few weeks before the 2020 American presidential election, I was so distraught, I could no longer think or pray. I withdrew into silence and solitude to maintain my sanity. Friends honored my decision and did not share their mounting anxiety with me. When it became clear that Joe Biden and Kamala Harris had won, a friend called to tell me that they would be speaking later that evening. When I tuned in, one of the CBC's American correspondents was interviewing people in the Maryland parking lot where Biden and Harris would later make their victory speeches. I was struck first by what was missing: the chest-thumping, fist-pumping, testosterone-driven crowing that follows the Super Bowl and a self-righteous smugness that had come to characterize American political-speak even before Trump ascended to the White House. I was struck by people's relief, their humility, their sanity and maturity, their focus on the work that lay ahead of them.

I was struck by Mr. Biden himself, the man neoliberal pundits had dismissed as "not presidential"—compared to what, they never said, exactly. What I heard was a man who spoke without rancor or recrimination, a leader calling for unity, not as a political strategy but from his heart because he had one. And for the first time in years, I heard a US politician speak not just of but directly to the soul of America because he knew it was still there, and he called us to be guided by our "better angels," echoing Abraham Lincoln's first inaugural address. And I prayed with all my heart that Americans were indeed still capable of doing the long, hard, slow, and unglamourous work of healing and reconciliation, because they are, for better or for worse, still my people.

Jill Johnston: An Unofficial Ubiquitary

Thespian lemonist, dance cricket, and irrepressible funster, Jill Johnston seemed to be everywhere in the 1970s—in The *Village Voice,* on The Dick Cavett Show, on the cover of *Life*. And then she wasn't. In 1987 she came up in a conversation I had with the poet Anne Witten on an island off the coast of Maine.

I pointed to her feet. "There's a photograph of Jill Johnston wearing boots just like that," I said.

"I knew Jill," said Anne. "In New York, in the old days. But I knew her lover Jane better. In fact, that's where Jill got most of her best lines."

Seven years later, I met Jane at Anne's funeral, and we got to laughing. Not that we were making merry over Anne's death from cancer, but we did a good bit of chuckling about the days that became known as the sexual revolution, a term probably coined by *Time.*

Jill once quoted the gay liberation chant (whose source is most likely *Plato's Symposium*): "An army of lovers cannot fail." To which Jane had responded: "An army of lovers can't get out of bed."

Then Jane told me that a publisher had once approached Jill to write a book about those years, the sixties and seventies in New York, but Jill had lost interest. She was on to something else and asked Jane if she would write it for her.

Jane said no thanks.

"Who remembers?" said Jane. "Was it Kate Millett who threw the jar of pickles at Ti-Grace, or did Ti-Grace throw the pickles at Kate Millett? Was it even pickles? It might have been anchovies. And what the hell was the argument about in the first place?"

Besides, the revolution was over.

My friend Kris introduced me to Johnston's *Village Voice* column in the seventies. We were students at Webster University outside St. Louis. Sometimes we couldn't even get out of the bookstore before she'd start reading it out loud, and we'd have to sit down on the floor and finish it—laughing and in awe. With titles like "The Genius I've Squandered in Bed," "R. D. Laing: The Misteek of Sighcosis," and "Tender Gluttons," her column was an event in our lives. Food for thought dropped by helicopters into a cultural famine. She was an ally. A big sister. A real sheroe, as Kris put it.

I bought a copy of Johnston's *Gullible's Travels,* a selection of her columns, before I left to teach in France in 1975, and I carried it all through Europe for two and a half years—dog-eared, coffee-stained, with tiny black marks on some of the pages where bits of burning tobacco had landed. Well read. Well loved.

Recently I went to a potluck supper in East Vancouver, a lively group of painters and cultural workers. A young woman, enthusiastic about all things Queer, said she'd never heard of Jill Johnston. Never mind. This woman is young enough to be Johnston's granddaughter, and as Johnston once said, "Telling it like it is means telling it like it was and how it is now that it isn't what it was to the is now people."

Feisty, irreverent, difficult, incomprehensible, surreal, as one critic put it, she was "part Gertrude Stein, part E. E. Cummings, with a dash of Jack Kerouac thrown in for good measure."

At midnight the day after her death, I still couldn't find an obituary anywhere but on her own website, where her lover, Ingrid, wrote: "May her liberated spirit guide us on our paths."

Theater

An actor's life for me.

The curtain rises on the fifth-grade class play at Community School. Tom Jackson plays King Arthur because he's the tallest boy. Slender, dark-haired Ken Krohner plays the handsome Lancelot. And I play his vengeful and cowardly sidekick, Sir Gawain.

Enter Lancelot and Gawain. Stage right.

Gawain: What ho! How the heck did a sword get stuck in that rock?

Lancelot: 'Tis the prophecy, my friend. Remember what Merlin said. He who pulls the sword from the stone shall be the rightful king.

Lancelot tries his hand but fails. Gawain grabs the sword with both hands, pulls, grunting, fails, then kicks the stone in disgust.

Lancelot: Come, Gawain. Let us go in search of Arthur.

Gawain rolls his eyes. They turn to exit, then see Arthur enter from the wings.

Arthur: What ho! Arthur approaches the stone and reads: Whomsoever pulleth this sword from this stone shall be the true and rightful King of England.

Arthur plants his feet wide apart, gets a good grip on the sword's hilt with both hands, takes a deep breath, and with every ounce of his considerable strength and virtue, slowly draws the sword up and out of the stone. Whereupon Lancelot drops to one knee and sweeps his hand from his shoulder to the ground in homage. Gawain rolls his eyes, gets down on one knee, and does the same.

I sit in one of five tall chairs with swivel seats at the Formica counter in our kitchen. I stare into a bowl of cornflakes beside a small plate with a piece of toast on it. I pretend that this is a rooming house owned by a kindly but clueless couple who are not our real parents. They give us room and board and provide my older siblings and me with a place to stay on our way to more interesting lives. In my mind, my brother is all set to become a star quarterback once he finishes high school. The younger of my two elder sisters will most likely become famous for her paint-by-number landscapes or as an internationally know dog trainer.

I'm thinking of my upcoming trip to Chicago with the Saturday-afternoon boys club I am in. I will very likely encounter a talent scout on the train. He'll spot me and say, "Hey kid. I can see you got what it takes." I practice looking surprised. "Me?" I'll say. "Yeah," he says, "you." The fact that the talent scout might be a child molester doesn't enter my mind. It's 1962. Or maybe it will happen later in the spring on the train to Briarcliff Manor, New York, where my eldest sister is enrolled in junior college, waiting for her big break as a fashion model in Manhattan. She's thin and pretty, like Audrey Hepburn. Either way, I know I'm destined to be a child star on Broadway.

It's just a matter of time.

I'm in a circle of a dozen or so other children, sitting on folding chairs in front of a stage at a makeshift acting school in a former dry-cleaning establishment in a strip mall on Delmar Boulevard. I'm the only boy. Mrs. Gold stands before us, one hand resting in the other just below her ample bosom.

"Welcome," she says, "to Junior Theater. The life you have chosen is by no means easy. It calls for commitment, discipline, and hard work. The rewards are many. A number of my students have become regular members of the summer singing and dancing choruses at the Muny Opera here in St. Louis. Others have gone on to study in Chicago and New York. A life in the theater takes grace and grit, and a willingness to make mistakes. One has to learn to accept disappointment, sometimes bitter and heartbreaking disappointment—and yet, really, there's nothing quite as fulfilling as . . ." Here her voice trails off. She looks up and off to her right for a long moment.

I hold my breath.

"Now!" she says, clapping her hands. We all jump. "The first exercise. I want each one of you to climb the stairs to the stage, turn, state your name, the grade you're in, the school you attend, and your favorite subject."

She makes her way, one sweeping step and then another, toward the windows of the storefront, curtains drawn against the glare from the parking lot. She strikes a pose as if ready to be photographed.

"Who will go first?"

We freeze, but just for a moment. Two girls, one blond, the other a redhead, race toward the steps and bump into each other.

"No, no, no, no," says Mrs. Gold. "This will never do. Go back to where you were. Both of you. Then proceed—slowly—toward the destination. Become aware of each other."

The girls return to their places and approach each other again, the blonde staring the redhead down. They stop at the stairs and look toward Mrs. Gold.

"Well?" she says. "Who's going to go first?"

The redhead bows slightly and says, "After you." The blonde thanks her and climbs the three steps to the stage, turns, stands erect, and says, "My name is Louise Schutzenhammer. I go to Flynn Park School. I'm in the sixth grade. And my favorite subject is reading."

Mrs. Gold nods. Louise returns to her seat.

The redhead takes to the stage next, squares her shoulders and announces: "My name is Mary Katherine McNally. I'm in the sixth grade at Visitation Academy. My favorite subjects are Latin, and comportment and elocution."

And so it goes until one girl states her name and then adds: "But my stage name is Betty Duval, and I'm going to get into the High School of Performing Arts in New York City even if it kills me."

A stage name. I hadn't thought of that. But then in my head I hear the voice of the snarkier of my two sisters saying: How about Little Lord Fauntleroy? She doesn't think much of my theatrical aspirations.

When it's my turn, I trudge up the stairs, turn around, and say my name, my school . . .

"Stop right there," says Mrs. Gold. "Look up. Speak out. I can barely hear you. Who are you?"

"Alfred DePew."

"Say it as if you mean it."

"Alfred DePew," I say louder, growing red in the face.

"Not like that. You sound irritated. Turn around three times and shake out your arms. Shake them out again. Now. Tell me who you are."

"I am Alfred DePew."

"Good," she says. "And?"

"I go to Community School. I'm in the sixth grade, and I like reading and music class."

"That's more like it," cries Mrs. Gold. "Now I want you all to pay attention. When you talk to somebody, look them in the eye. Say what you have to say. And notice how they hear it. You are trying to communicate something. And you want to be heard—and understood."

My heart catches in my throat. She has named the two things I want most in the world. And maybe—just maybe—she can teach me how to get them.

"What do you mean, you can't go back?" asks my mother. "You begged us to let you do this. We paid good money."

I don't tell her that I can't learn my lines and am paralyzed by fear.

"I just can't," I say in my most desperate voice. "I just can't," I repeat more softly. For effect.

My mother rolls her eyes, which is where I picked up the habit.

We've reached our usual impasse. I squirm. I wiggle. I complain of a sore throat—probably laryngitis, maybe even strep throat.

My mother gives up. She has errands to run.

Next year, I am in seventh grade and in the Junior Chorus at the combined junior high/high school I will attend for the next six years. My stage fright is intense. In a chorus, I can blend in, fade, drop back, except I'm short and so they always put me in the front row. Nevertheless, I'm not alone out there.

We're rehearsing *Finian's Rainbow*, this year's spring musical, in the outdoor amphitheater. "A robust full-throated ensemble crowd scene," the drama teacher explains. I'm a little lost, but I follow the other boys who step forward and to the left. The soloist sings. We lean in with our left hand on our knee and our right hand on our hip and then sing out with all the masculine vigor we can muster: *"This time of the year!"* In a few bars, we have some high-stepping dance moves, thumbs hitched in our imaginary suspenders, moving our elbows up and down. Mr. Arnold, the drama teacher, reminds us that we are salt-of-the-earth farmers. "Robust" and "vigorous" are two of his favorite words. But the fact remains, we're in a white suburb of St. Louis, about as far away from the salt of the earth as you can get and still be on the same planet.

The truth is, we look like chickens flapping our wings.

Two years later I stand by the piano in the music room, holding a sheet with the words to the song the teacher wants me to sing as my audition for the role of Lord High Executioner in *The Mikado,* this year's spring musical. The role makes me think of my sister's stories about dances at her junior college when the lights would flicker, go out, and then come back on again because someone at the state penitentiary four miles up the road was getting fried in the electric chair. I'm flattered to have been asked to audition, and some part of me still hopes this might be the break I've been waiting for, but I'm haunted by performance anxiety and have nightmares of stepping out onto a stage in my pajamas—or worse—buck naked.

The music teacher plays the song again, so that I might come closer to getting it right this time. My voice has changed. I'm still a tenor, but I squeak now and then. My family is in crisis. And I'm failing algebra. So I withdraw from the auditions, citing my need to focus on academics.

I fail algebra anyway and have to go to summer school, which gives me time to think. Maybe the actor's life isn't for me after all. Maybe I'm a writer, which feels safer, somehow. Private. Easier to hide and work at correcting my mistakes.

The following year I discover the backstage world of high-school theatrical productions, helping the scene painters after school. Kids a couple of years ahead of me have formed a kind of bohemian subculture that will serve as a bridge from the beatniks to the hippies—an alternative to bonehead jocks, egghead nerds, and manic cheerleaders, many of whom, after a few beers, reveal a troubling mean streak.

I learn about the world east of Skinker Boulevard—jazz clubs, coffeehouses, poets, underground newspapers, abstract painters, and a certain eccentric bookseller who has befriended one of the boys in particular.

It's backstage that my friend Jake discovers that a ladder outside the second-story dressing rooms leads to a trapdoor that opens into a crawl space, where we explore some of what we have been warned to avoid by our sex education teacher, who, we suspect, doesn't know a whole lot more about it than we do.

Once in college, my interest shifts to twentieth-century novels, European cinema, music history, and psychology, until I discover that the behaviorists have hijacked American psychology, and I drop it. My real subject of study is, of course, life, which I decide to observe in the tradition of Collette, Proust, and Virginia Woolf. I watch everyone very carefully, recording quirks, oddities, alliances, and betrayals in cardboard-covered lab books from the college bookstore.

Beloit College has a work-study program, which places students in jobs and internships all over the world. I choose a bookstore in Cambridge, England, because my French isn't good enough to work in France.

I rent a room at the top of a house on Mill Road, a half-hour walk from Bowes & Bowes at 1 Trinity Street. My wage is ten pounds, ninety-seven pence, handed to me in a brown envelope by the bookkeeper each Friday. I have no coursework for the next three months. I can smoke cigarettes and drink warm beer with strange particles floating in it to my heart's content, and I have access to hundreds—thousands—of books and plenty of time to read.

Surely my real life has begun.

After work, a group of us troop off to the Eagle, the preferred watering hole of shop clerks, aspiring poets, and stagehands and carpenters from the Arts Theatre around the corner, not to mention the odd mental patient out on a day pass from the nearby minimum security hospital. There I sit, keen to observe them all from a safe distance. But not for long. It may be the beer—the floating bits might be hallucinogenic—but before I know it, I am in some kind of love triangle or parallelogram spinning at full tilt. My friend Rupert, one of the carpenters, is in love with a married man who is currently one of the mental patients, a regular fellow, Rupert assures me, who has just hit a rough patch, and who qualifies for the occasional day pass and brings along with him a woman who is honest-to-god crazy. Other characters include the barmaid and her old friend Geraldine, recently returned from Canada and looking for work, which she finally finds at the theater.

Down the unrequited love spiral Rupert descends, and I follow, determined to save him from himself, for, without realizing it, I seem to be in love with him. So I am sucked into the vortex of what I think might one day make a good novel.

Rupert gets us tickets for the current Arts Theatre production of *The Bacchae,* Euripides's play about King Pentheus and his mother who run afoul of Dionysus, the god of the vine, religious ecstasy, madness, and theater. The production is daring in the sprit of the early '70s. Women in body stockings writhe in the frenzy of ritual. Departing from classical Greek tradition, the murder is performed in full view, front and center, close enough for blood to splatter Rupert's green velvet jacket. Not real blood of course. This is regional theater on a tight budget. It's water-based paint and easy enough to wash out, but unsettling nonetheless and it sends poor Rupert into another tailspin from which he does, in time, recover.

Meanwhile, my work visa runs out, and I return to the States to finish my undergraduate degree at Webster University outside St. Louis, whose English Department, as fate would have it, is housed on the ground floor along one edge of the theater complex. Like it or not, I have been drawn into the archetypal field of Dionysus and there's no way out. I seem to think I can navigate all this and find my way around actors in breastplates and rags and flowing gowns in the hallway waiting for their entrance as I proceed to my exam in eighteenth-century British literature. I step cautiously and remain outside the world of theater.

I cannot, however, seem to avoid the theater of the world and keep getting drawn into the political drama which I entered when I registered with the Selective Service as a conscientious objector when I turned eighteen. It's now three years later, the war is "winding down," my number in the first lottery is very high and so I have no fear of being drafted, but the world keeps calling for a response. No matter how hard I try to stay out of it, to remain detached and observe, I am in it. I fancy myself a fellow traveler of Trotskyists, poets, lesbian separatists, and the lumpenproletariat. I fall in and out of love, drift from one bar to another, total my car, get arrested for drunk driving, and resume work with a therapist. I live parallel lives as a student, a barfly, an imaginary revolutionist, a middle-class white boy who still lives with his parents in the suburbs, an aspiring writer who's much too busy gathering material to write much of anything.

Somehow I manage to graduate and am awarded a teaching internship in a high school in northern France, where I learn about World War II by living in a small city that had been leveled by German bombers and hearing the lived experience of people during the war. I've learned about the war in school, but somehow I need to learn about it in my body as I walk through fields that were once full of land mines and that still have remnants of concrete blockhouses for snipers. I have to walk through ruins of the star-shaped fortress wall designed by Vauban in the seventeenth century on my way to the post office in town. I learn about the social and moral dilemmas of my Moroccan students, who, though born in France, are still considered foreign, not only by their fellow citizens but also by their own families. I learn about the crucial role of the French Communist Party in the Resistance and the ongoing resentment against those who collaborated with the Nazis farther to the south. This is what I have to learn: That everyone—including me—has been ravaged by the war.

At the end of the school year, I migrate back to England and find work in a summer school teaching English to Spanish kids. I reconnect with Geraldine, who has become the administrative assistant to the general manager of Cambridge Theatre Company. One day, I stop by the office to give her a message, but she hasn't returned from lunch, so her boss invites me to have a seat in the office they share and wait for her. He turns back to his work, and I pull the *Herald Tribune* from my backpack and read the front page. After a time, I put the paper down and turn to the man behind the desk.

"What do you suppose will happen in China now that Mao Zedong is dead?"

The man looks at me with a startled expression, somewhere between peevish and provoking, and says, "I'm quite sure I don't know. What's more, I can't say as I care."

"How can you not care?" I cry. "A quarter of the earth's population lives in China."

He gives me a look I find hard to read, which I come to understand is meant to convey British superiority and contempt, but this is mixed with challenge and a sneering lechery, as if in one glance he has stripped me naked.

I lift the paper and open it to page two. I am flummoxed. I decide to wait until my heart stops racing and the deep blush drains from my face. If Geraldine is not back in five minutes, I'll excuse myself and leave. After what seems like the right amount of time, I look at my watch and say I really must be going and would he mind telling Geraldine that I stopped by?

"Who shall I say was calling?"

"Just tell her that Alf came by. It isn't anything urgent. I'll catch up with her later."

"Alf," he says. "I'm Chris." And he extends his hand across the desk. I give it a quick firm shake, smile awkwardly, and take pains not to walk too fast out the door and down the stairs, though, in truth, I want to run.

When I see her again, Geraldine says I've made quite an impression on Christopher, and he wants to have dinner with me. He persists, through Geraldine, and some weeks later, I relent.

Once inside the Italian restaurant—and after a few drinks—I begin to let my guard down. Chris is being authentically and genuinely charming, so there is something underneath all that bluff and bluster. And before I know it, I'm telling him my life story—twenty-four years of wounded idealism, knee-jerk opinions about the world, outrage, magical thinking, denial: you name it. And he listens. He seems interested.

And I am smitten—Mrs. Gold's words from Junior Theater ringing in my ears: to be heard . . . and understood.

After dinner we go to the flat he shares with a colleague who also travels for work and is out of town. Soon enough we are dozing in each other's arms. Chris wakes with a start and gets up to dress. I keep trying to pull him back into bed. He has to drive to London for an Arts Council meeting later in the day.

He gives me a lift back to Holland Street, where I am staying, and off he goes. We don't see much of each other in what remains of the summer, but come fall, we write letters back and forth once I've found another teaching job and am settled in a town about an hour and a half north of Barcelona by train.

Like the city in northern France where I lived the year before, Figueres had been heavily bombed not only throughout World War II but also during the Spanish Civil War, Catalonia being the last province to fall to Franco's forces in 1939. Once again I am inducted into a historical drama I know nothing about.

After Franco bans the public use of Catalan, newspapers and books in the language nearly disappear. By the time I arrive in the fall of 1976, many of my ESL students at the British Institute are also enrolled in Catalan classes and poets and writers are beginning to publish again, having been silenced for nearly forty years.

Though Franco has been dead for almost twelve months, his armed police force, *los grises,* continue to roam the streets, ready to repress any opposition to the Francoist regime. Lluís Llach, a Catalan folk singer living in exile in France, comes to Figueres to give a concert. Our students at the British Institute invite us to attend, so the director and I make our way with crowds of others through phalanxes of military police, some on horseback. It is not a large city and this is not a large venue, certainly not by North American standards. We are directed to our seats in the first balcony, and when our students see us, they stand and start cheering, explaining to the people around them who we are—foreigners, English teachers, allies, friends. That we are there is an act of solidarity. To this day, I can't explain the sense of kinship I felt for these people whom I hardly knew, whose language I didn't speak, and whose history I was only beginning to learn. When Llach comes to a song he is expressly forbidden to sing in Spain, he plays the first few bars on the piano, and the audience sings it for him. They know it by heart. I may not understand the words, but the love and grief and outrage are unmistakable, for we are all—literally—in it together. Theater without an audience is just another rehearsal. It depends on us for life and we—our lives, our cultural lives, our communal lives and identity—depend on theater.

My letters to Chris are full of the political tensions I am trying to understand. His letters are full of the challenges he's encountering as the new general manager of Britain's largest touring company while it seeks to make the Old Vic its London base. Geraldine remains his administrative assistant.

I leave Catalonia just before the first general election to be held since the Spanish Civil War. There is no telling what might happen and many fear the Fascists will try to seize power if they don't like the results. King Juan Carlos has been a stabilizing influence, but it's anybody's guess.

I can't afford to fly back to London, so I take a bus. Chris agrees to meet me at Victoria Station and I arrive bedraggled and badly frightened. I'm headed back to Cambridge to teach ESL to the children of wealthy *madrileños* who've shipped their kids to England for a month, so they can go on holiday without them—that's how it seems to me, at least. I have some compassion for them even though I know many of their parents are Fascist sympathizers.

I am back and forth to London every other weekend. Chris and I are both on edge, trying to navigate the next step in our individual lives and trying to find a way of being together. I'm looking for a job on the Continent for the fall; he's still getting settled into his job at the Old Vic. In August I get a rejection letter from a language school in Denmark, but an Italian school wants an interview—in London. The Italian school doesn't hire me either. Why would they come all the way to London to hire an American, though I like to think my English is passable. I've softened my consonants, opened my vowels. Not exactly BBC quality, but surely good enough for Italians just beginning to learn English. Apparently not. I have two more weeks left at my job in Cambridge, and then I don't know what.

"Come to London," says Chris. "You can stay here for a while. And Priscilla needs help in the publicity department. We could pay you out of petty cash—since you're an illegal alien." He grins a half grin, free of contempt.

One of my first jobs in the publicity office is to answer Derek Jacobi's fan mail. Partly due to the success of the BBC television series *I, Claudius,* Jacobi has become the heartthrob of nearly every fourteen-year-old girl, and any number of boys, in Britain.

"Dear Miss Witherspoon," I write and look up asking, "What the hell kind of name is that?" To no answer. Priscilla is busy typing news releases on a manual typewriter, which is why I am writing in longhand on a pad of paper before I copy it onto a sheet of Prospect Theatre Company stationary. "Thank you ever so much for" I cross that out and begin again.

> *Thank you for your letter of 12 September. There is not, as far as I know, a fan club for Mr. Jacobi, so you may want to start one in your area. And as to your request for an autographed picture, I am afraid I can't be of much help there either.*
>
> *Should you have the opportunity to travel to London and attend a performance of Hamlet, you might want to try your luck at the stage door after the final curtain.*

Please know that Mr. Jacobi appreciates your enthusiastic support, as do we all here at the Old Vic.

I remain yours, most sincerely,

Alfred DePew
Publicity Assistant
Prospect Theatre Company at the Old Vic

One day the regular receptionist calls in sick, so I am put on the switchboard downstairs, which is pretty simple—a call comes in, I answer by plugging the receiver cord into the jack that's lit up, ask to whom the caller would like to speak, then plug the sending cord into the appropriate jack, push the lever on the desk forward, and the two parties talk to their hearts' content.

A call comes in from someone trying to get free tickets, pretending to work for the Queen. What does he take me for, stupid? "Yeah, right," I say and pull the cord out of the jack.

Ten minutes later, Chris comes flying through the door.

"Did you just hang up on Buckingham Palace?"

"You mean—I thought it was a prank call."

"This is *England*, Alf. *London*. That's where Buckingham Palace *is*. Her Majesty is one of our *patrons*, for Chrissake!"

Before I can offer to call them and apologize, he has stormed back through the door. A few minutes later, Geraldine relieves me of my duty, shaking her head and sniggering.

I go back to the publicity office. Priscilla laughs when I tell her—she's Australian, so she kind of gets it. But I've done nothing to improve our relationship with the general manager, that is Chris, with whom I am now living, which we are trying to downplay to avoid accusations of favoritism, which is of course what it is.

Next, I am put in charge of a poster-design contest for London area schools as part of our publicity campaign for the Christmas pantomime. Submissions arrive in wax crayon and colored markers and I stack and sort. Priscilla and I narrow them down to half a dozen and then choose the winning design, which will be made into the front-of-house poster and appear in newspaper ads.

We hold a press conference onstage at lunchtime and serve drinks, quite a few drinks. I am nervous, and each time the server comes by, I take another glass of wine. I have nothing to say about the pantomime or the competition that isn't already in the press release, and nobody really cares, so I listen to first one and then another journalist tell stories, and try to remain upright on the steeply raked stage. I smile. I nod. And I keep knocking back glasses of cheap wine.

When I get back to the office, I sit down to the work I have to finish by day's end, but everything swims before my eyes, and I start to cry. Priscilla puts her hand on my shoulder and tries to reassure me with something that she says is Buddhist: "You are not your opinion of yourself."

"That may well be," I say, "but I'm still too drunk to work."

At which point I throw up on a pile of contest submissions, but not—thank God—the winner and two runners-up, which have been copied and are safely in the press packets we've just handed out.

The drama in the streets grows more intense. Gangs of skinheads attack people of color. Fights break out on trains after football matches. People in mixed-race and working-class districts get fliers through their letter slots warning "wogs" to get out of Britain and go back where they came from. An undercurrent of violence and menace pervades the city.

I stand at the second-floor widows with the general office staff, watching men in brown shirts and leather jackets turn off of Waterloo Road onto The Cut and march by us, calling for the deportation of all foreigners. When I say how frightened I am by this, Geraldine quips, "They don't mean you, Alf. You're white."

I don't know what troubles me more: the hatred of people marching in the street or the complacency of my colleagues in the theater. I think of my nine months in not-yet-post-Fascist Spain, under the constant watch of military police patrolling the streets with their rifles. I think of my Catalan students and neighbors, their deep faith and high spirits, their determination to emerge from under an occupation that still oppresses them. Their moves are cautious yet persistent. Tense doesn't describe the atmosphere. Electric is more like it—fear and courage rubbing against each other, generating light.

In Spain, we talked about what was going on.

Here in London, I'm engulfed by an insidious silence.

In a fit of pique, the actress playing Ophelia cuts up all her wigs after a performance and goes home to sulk. The next day *Vogue* calls, wanting to interview her because she's getting rave reviews.

"What do I tell them?" I whisper to Priscilla, my hand over the mouthpiece.

"Tell them she's indisposed, a bit under the weather, and we'll ring them back when she's feeling better."

Suppliers go unpaid; we struggle to make payroll week to week. The set for *Hamlet* will not travel, so a separate touring set has to be designed—and paid for. The actress playing Joan of Arc next season insists that we airbrush the wrinkles out of her face on the photo we are using for the posters. Priscilla caves in, and so there's that expense as well. Despite consistently good reviews, ticket sales are sluggish. There are grumblings from every quarter, and tensions are running high.

Geraldine and I sit drinking in the wine bar in a dark and irritable funk. She makes a snide remark, and I snap, "You're useless, worse than useless. You need to resign." Geraldine storms out of the bar in tears. I sit and stew for a while. Then Chris pokes his head around the corner, says he'll bring the car around front and to meet him outside.

I stand in a cold, wet wind, taking deep breaths, shaking my arms out, trying to sober up a bit. Once in the passenger seat, I look straight ahead and say, "Promise me you won't get angry."

"What have you done now?"

"Promise first."

"Well it can't be worse than hanging up on Buckingham Palace."

"I'm afraid it is. I just fired Geraldine."

"You *what*?"

"You promised you wouldn't get mad."

"What made you think—"

"I know. I know. She made me angry. I'll talk to her in the morning and apologize. I'm so sorry."

"What is the matter with you?"

"I don't know," I whisper.

We drive home in silence and sleep in separate rooms that night.

Chris is in the bathtub, his eyes closed, steam rising all around him. I sit on the floor. He's trying to relax, so I'm not talking, which is hard. I want to apologize, make things right again. His hand rests on the edge of the tub. I stare at the nicotine stains on the inside of his index and middle fingers. He has the hands of a surgeon or a priest. One who works with sacred vessels or sharp tools, which he uses with precision. He knows how to disassemble the engine of his 1965 MG MGB, clean or replace the parts, and put the whole thing back together again. I've watched him do it on a Sunday afternoon. He has a genius for keeping things in good running order. I remember everything I love about him and much of what makes me impatient.

"I really am sorry, Chris."

"Oh please," he says with his eyes still closed. "Let's not talk about it again."

"All right. It's just that—I'm on your side. I really am."

"You have odd ways of showing it," he says, opening one eye and giving me a half smile.

"Everything's going to be all right. You know that, don't you?"

"If you say so."

"I know so."

For I know without fully knowing that I have to leave London. I'm tired of witty repartee, caustic rejoinders, and bitchy jibes, as if we were all caught in a Noël Coward nightmare.

It's time to go home. Having seen recently the New York cast of *A Chorus Line* and Julie Harris in *The Belle of Amherst,* I am moved in ways I hadn't expected. Homesick for the tension between those two poles in the American spirit—extroverted, determined, even aggressive optimism on the one hand; on the other, silence, isolation, and the "ruin" that lies "within" as Emily Dickinson reminds us. I have to come to terms with these fragments and facets of the American soul and in my own.

After I complete my graduate studies in American literature, I settle in Portland, Maine, where I cobble together enough part-time teaching jobs to pay rent and buy food. Prospect Theatre Company doesn't survive. Chris finds other work in theater administration. We continue to write to each other, and some years later, he pays me a visit while he's on a holiday tour of the States. We've both lost parents and are finding our way though grief, which connects us more deeply than ever before. In February 1992, I receive an envelope from the UK. My address is written in a hand I don't recognize, and I have an uneasy feeling as I carry it upstairs to my apartment. The letter inside from someone I don't know tells me Chris is dead—of cancer, discovered in the lung, treated, and then discovered in the bone. All in a matter of weeks. She is writing, she says, because she found my last letter on his desk.

It takes me a while to catch up to what is happening, as if I have been lifted out of time and left floating in midair. Again, I know without knowing how I know even before I open the envelope that Christopher is dead, and my life will never be quite the same. Yet I can't fit the parts together. Something that I didn't realize I depended upon being solid has dissolved, and I start searching everywhere for his last letter. I'm not even sure I realize how much this means, how much Chris has meant. And now some essential connection to that part of my past, my life, and the world itself has been severed. Somehow I have been widowed without knowing I'd ever been married.

Twenty-four years later, when I hear that Glenda Jackson is to play Lear at the Old Vic, everything in my body says: Go! I book flights, buy theater tickets, and arrange to see the few people I still know in England.

I'm standing in Waterloo Station. Dusty gray light drifts down through the massive skylight. It's November, just before

Remembrance Day. Veterans sell paper poppies from a small kiosk in the middle of the floor. I buy one and stick it into my coat lapel. People stream around me, in a hurry to catch their train. I stand still. I don't know what year it is. 1977? 1920? 1939? Sometime between wars, the last one and the next, which I can almost feel approaching, a sudden moistness against my neck that makes me shiver. I brush it away with my hand and remind myself that it's 2016. I'm sixty-four years old. I live in Canada. I have come to see Glenda Jackson play King Lear in a theater where I worked for a short time in another life.

Waterloo Station is full of ghosts: shell-shocked men with bandaged heads, refugees from Spain, from Poland, Germany, the Netherlands. Ghosts clutching bundles and the hands of their young children, ghosts carrying the weight of betrayals, in search of some sane and moral ground to stand on once again. They follow me like a dark mist, a winding sheet.

The Old Vic looks smaller than I remember. Some part of me thinks I will find Chris in the upstairs office that overlooks the marquee and Geraldine sitting in the wine bar. But they too are ghosts.

An usher shows me to my seat in the stalls, next to two schoolteachers who've come up to London from Worthing. They tell me that Boris Johnson sits four rows ahead of us. I've been avoiding all news for weeks because of the upcoming American elections.

"Remind me who he is."

"A two-faced lying traitor is who he is," she says, raising her voice. People turn to look at us.

I remember now. The television personality. A columnist. Brexit.

A man walks onstage, pushing a broom. Someone else carries a chair and puts it down. Out of these movements, the play begins, as if it has been going on for centuries. The stage is bare, the costumes minimal. Jackson wears trousers; a red tunic signifies Lear's sovereignty. Lear's daughters wear American-style pantsuits. The Fool sports a Superman shirt.

However sparse the set and costumes, the language remains untouched, more potent, more poignant than I remember. Something about Jackson's twenty-three years in Parliament lends a weight, edge, and authority to Lear's political speeches that few actors can convey.

I am pulled into the dreaming, in and out of time, moving through a broad spectrum that—weirdly—includes the future.

For this is the eve of the American election that will put Donald Trump in the White House. In three years, Boris Johnson will be the prime minister of Britain. Vladimir Putin and his oligarchs have ruled Russia for sixteen years already. These men contaminate with their greed what will come to be known as our history, our legacy to future generations.

I think of Lenin's famous cry: "What is to be done?"

And Hamlet's answer: "Speak the speech, I pray you . . . Suit the action to the word, the word to the action . . . And let those that play your clowns speak no more than is set down for them."

A silence follows the Duke of Albany's last speech. Then applause. We rise and make our way to the exits, still in the thrall of a dream we carry into the night outside, pulling the collar of our coat close against the chill. We hail a taxi, cross the street to catch a train—a dream we won't remember, yet which persists, just below the level of our waking consciousness, persists and moves in us as we dig into a pocket, grasp the latchkey, and open the door to sleep.

An old Jesuit friend says: If liturgy doesn't disturb us in some way, it's not doing its job. And so it is with theater. Whether through madcap laughter or terror and pity, we are unsettled, changed somehow, not the same people who took our seats before the curtain rose. We have been in the dangerous presence of a wild, elusive truth, seeking its freedom in a space large enough to contain angels, demons, daemons, and gods. A place we return to again and again to be redeemed when we fail at the fitful, frightening work of love.

Pilgrimage

I am circling around God, around the ancient tower
and I have been circling for a thousand years,
and I still don't know if I am a falcon, or a storm,
or a great song.

—Rainer Maria Rilke
(trans. Robert Bly)

"So," says Sister Pat, "you're interfaith."

We're sitting in her office in a retreat center on Vancouver Island. I am new to the Catholic Church and even newer to Canada, having landed in British Columbia seven weeks earlier. This is my first retreat, and Sister Pat is my first spiritual director. Twenty years of Sufi teachings and practices had reconciled me with the Christian tradition from which I had become estranged as a teenager during the Vietnam War. Sufism also led to my study of the Torah with a rabbi when I lived in Maine. When I described to him my desire to heal the rifts in the Abrahamic line, I asked if there were some initiation or ceremony that might help me. He suggested a mikvah, a ritual cleansing, but as we talked further, it became clear that I had no intention of renouncing other wisdom traditions or abandoning their practices.

"Let me get this straight," he said. "You plan on continuing to take Communion after you become a Jew?"

"That's correct."

"Well for God's sake don't tell the other rabbis."

All of which I convey to Sister Pat, half expecting her to tell me to give up this nonsense and promise never to do it again. Instead, she says, "It looks like you're going to have to live it."

"Yes," I say. "I see . . . but how?"

"That," she says, "is between you and the Holy Spirit."

When I get back to Vancouver, a friend asks what new insights or guidance I have received from my retreat.

I shrug. "Await further instructions?"

When describing the way to reach the notoriously hard-to-find Haystack Mountain School of Crafts, the poet and potter M. C. Richards said, "Forget easy access. Think pilgrimage." I've always liked that, but I'm not sure it's the right word for what I'm on. Pilgrimage assumes a destination: Santiago de Compostela, Mecca, Jerusalem, some place you get to and then return home from. Mine feels more like wandering in the desert, seeking refuge, finding it for a time, then setting out once more. Indigenous people sometimes say they feel sorry for the descendants of European settlers. They say we have no home. They say we are always on our way to somewhere else—heaven, nirvana—and that's why we're so restless, always in a hurry, always disappointed. They wonder why we keep looking over our left shoulder as if we still feel the hot breath of those who drove us into exile—as if we could outrun history, leave the ancestors behind, put what they suffered far from our minds, forget what they held sacred and what they saw destroyed. They may not know we had so little warning, fled with only what we could carry or sew into our clothes, sometimes forced to leave children in what we prayed were safe circumstances.

Aimless though it has often seemed to me and appeared to others, there is purpose to my wandering and has been from the very start—sparked by a desire God placed in my heart before I was born. I follow a path that makes itself known to me only if I keep on walking.

On my father's side, I am descended from Huguenots who fled France some months before the St. Bartholomew's Day massacre in 1572 and which is said to have resulted in the deaths of between five and thirty thousand people. One legend has it that my forebear Bartholomew DuPuy was visited one evening by the village priest who advised him to convert—the sooner, the better. Bowing one's head to Rome was preferable to having it cut off. Bartholomew took the hint, gathered his family, packed whatever they could carry on two horses, and headed toward what is now Germany, then to Amsterdam, a city providing safe haven for French Protestants and Jews fleeing the Spanish Inquisition. In another version of the story, we stayed in France until the revocation of the Edict of Nantes in 1685, when we joined between two hundred and nine hundred thousand others who left France.

In any case, my branch of the family made their way to the New World via England, where we were given refuge for a while. Some settled in upstate New York. Others continued west to St. Louis, where they became mostly Unitarians and Christian Scientists. My mother came from English Quakers, Scots-Irish Presbyterians, nonconformists, and abolitionists.

Not a papist on either side of the family for generations, so you can imagine the response I got when I was eight years old and announced at dinner one evening that my birthday, March 25, fell on the Feast of the Annunciation.

"What the heck is that?" asked my sister Carol.

"It's when Archangel Gabriel came to Mary and told her she was going to give birth to Jesus," I explained.

"Honestly," said our eldest sister, Ann, rolling her eyes. Our brother, Charles, started laughing so hard that milk came out of his nose, and my mother sent him to the kitchen to fetch something to clean it up with.

"You're lying!" cried Carol.

"I am not!" I yelled.

"Now, now," said our father. "We'll have none of that." He rose from his seat, went to the living room, and came back with the first volume of the World Book Encyclopedia. "Let's see," he said. "Annunciation. Well what do you know? Alfred is right."

Many years later, when I began to pray with the Annunciation by imagining myself in the scene, I felt like an intruder, sneaking a peak at something that, as a man, I had no business seeing—a profoundly feminine intimacy. I would imagine myself outside, peering in through a window, or in another part of the room, out of Mary's range of vision. No matter where I stood, I felt like a spy. In one prayer period, I found myself hovering in midair. I heard faint sounds from the earth below, and as I came nearer, I saw people tilling the soil. Others were fighting and killing each other. To my left, I noticed a large white light, expanding and contracting. An amorphous shape started to emerge as it made its descent toward Mary, who sat on a stool and looked up in wonder as she became aware of the angel.

Whether or not I feel I should be there, I keep being called to bear witness to the encounter between Gabriel and Mary. Pay attention, God seems to be saying, this is part of your sacred story.

When I was six or seven, my next-door neighbor and best friend, a Catholic, informed me that I was going to hell because I was a Protestant. "There's no such place," said my mother. "Everybody goes to heaven." But who was right? Was there a hell or not? And who got to go to heaven and who didn't? And if you don't go to heaven, where else is there? And how come Ditty Weinrich had a guardian angel and I didn't? There I was, not even eight years old and dropped into the religious wars of the sixteenth, seventeenth, and eighteenth centuries, maybe my first awareness of slippage in the time-space continuum, an experience that was to become more familiar to me in the years that followed.

I never had to think about God before I started going to Sunday school. Until then, God just was. The world—my world—was full of magic: color, sound, sensation, puppies, big people, a duck pond, and a long sloping hill to the woods. A world of wonder I toddled, then walked, then ran through. Music from somewhere. The presence of sprites and angels—unseen by others but making themselves known to me, and none of them frightening. Grown-ups kept asking me if what I was describing was "real" or "make-believe." I didn't understand the difference, but learned to tell them what they wanted to hear. As I was being inducted into their way of seeing and thinking, I felt the world as I knew it recede, and I began to worry. The beings known only to me began to disappear, which is to say I lost touch with them, but they stayed close at hand, as I found out later.

At Sunday school, I learned about this fellow Jesus, who had a lot of good advice about staying out of trouble. I was asked to trade in my living God for one in a picture book. I was bored, but I needed to know what was expected of me. And nobody seemed to be able to tell me who was right, the Catholics or the Protestants, and what about the Jewish kids? Who told them how to behave? History lessons only made things worse. Everyone was trying to kill each other for no apparent reason. Something called human nature was to blame, and that's why we needed Jesus, who didn't seem to me to be doing a very good job of controlling people's behavior. I couldn't keep my questions to myself, and I made everybody nervous. Meanwhile, the world around us was splitting apart. People calling for an end to racial segregation were met with fire hoses and attack dogs, Black churches were torched by white supremacists, and young men, calling for an end to the Vietnam War, burned their draft cards. My heart rose and broke open with the Civil Rights marchers, and I felt called to the peace movement, not just because I was facing military conscription but because, according to Jesus, war—in fact violence of any kind—was indefensible.

Turns out Jesus was the last person to hang out with if you wanted to avoid trouble.

The first time I consulted an astrologer, she suggested that I'd had a number of lifetimes in which I was "lightly incarnated," as if I'd been watching myself from the wings.

"It's like those bumper cars at the amusement park," she said. "You bought your ticket, got into a car, and then did your best to avoid touching any of the other cars. But that's the whole point of the ride—to run into each other."

I knew exactly what she meant, but I didn't have a clue about how to shed my aversion to bumping.

Luckily, eighteen months later, the earth opened and swallowed me whole. My father died, and I was pitched headlong into the shadowy realm of the dead. The world was wrapped in gauze. The air—viscous and heavy. He died at the end of March, and when signs of spring began to appear some weeks later, the sight of those first forsythia blossoms was unbearable. How could things bloom when I was dead inside, cut off from a root I didn't even know I had, in a world I refused to fully enter? And how could I be in the grip of this howling anguish over the loss of something I never felt was mine?

I was depressed. That's what everyone told me.

"I don't think it's depression in the clinical sense," said my new therapist. "What you're in is what we call grief."

I started to notice how strenuously I avoided my emotions. Intermittent periods of numbness involved in the grieving process were one thing. This was something else. Since my father had been a recovering alcoholic, my therapist suggested I go to an Al-Anon meeting. "All you have to do is breathe," she said. "And listen." I gathered my courage and walked into a room full of people I had spent the last fifteen years trying to get away from—my family of origin. But here they were telling the truth about how crazy it was and how much pain they were in. My heart raced. I broke into a cold sweat. I knew exactly what they were talking about, but I couldn't admit that it had anything to do with me. My body was telling me a different story. I left the meeting in turmoil. In the year that followed, a growing awareness of my own dependence on alcohol led me to AA, which I found even more terrifying than Al-Anon. And yet, in some strange way, it was a relief. There was a way out. Recovery was a reality.

Once I stopped medicating with alcohol, a sharp pain in my left shoulder and the base of my neck became so pronounced, I sought out a chiropractor and then a massage therapist, whose treatments opened me to a deeper experience of my emotions, which seemed, at the same time, to open me even more to Spirit. In ways I didn't understand or even believe were possible, I was gradually being knit back together, releasing fear, resentment, and envy, and finding some measure of comfort in my own skin.

Early in my second year of recovery, I was overwhelmed with fears I couldn't shake. I was able to make it to work each day and to AA meetings, but I was too afraid to do anything else. I prayed each morning to a God I didn't really think was there, and spoke up in AA meetings, but nothing seemed to help. My sponsor pointed to my relationship with my higher power and asked me to describe who or what I thought I was praying to. It turned out the best image I could come up with was an alcoholic parent—largely absent, undependable, whose mood could turn on a dime. No one you'd choose to trust with the keys to your car or the care of a small child. Find a higher power you can actually trust, said my sponsor. When I reviewed my first two years of recovery I came to understand that my actual experience of divine reality—its abundant love and possibilities—had grown so deep and wide that my old notions about God had shattered; I was in a kind of void, a state of suspended animation, an empty place, which I found terrifying because it was so unfamiliar. Little by little, God was something I could lean into, and that made the world larger and more possible.

A lot was coming together in my life. I sold an essay to *New Age Journal* and another to the *Maine Sunday Telegram.* I wrote radio spots as a freelancer for a local ad agency. I wrote fiction and was awarded an artist fellowship from the Maine Arts Commission. I was healing—physically, mentally, emotionally, and spiritually. Then there was the question of sex.

There's a sort of unspoken norm to which recovering drunks point themselves. The twelve steps of Alcoholics Anonymous urge us to accept "life on life's terms," which conformed to the assumed cultural norms of the men who wrote them in the1930s: white, middle-class, Christian, North American. One of the things I love about drunks is that most of us cannot seem to conform to social usage even when we're sober. Our most ardent attempts to imitate conventional behavior are all too often ridiculous. That's why you hear us laughing so hard at ourselves in AA meetings. And it has everything to do with the rigorous honesty we are called to practice in working the twelve steps.

To be sure, there were good and helpful discussions about aligning our sexual choices and behavior with sober living in the contemporary world. And there was sound guidance about ethics and safe sex practices. Cognitive psychology was a great help, but it could only go so far. Conventional massage, acupuncture, and other forms of energy work were also healing and deeply integrative, but something was missing for me—and I didn't know what it was.

Desire itself had become contaminated by addiction. How could I experience my desire and not pick up a drink or a drug? Part of it, of course, had to do with being vulnerable—even with myself. So much of my life had involved fleeing the body, resisting, protecting, shutting down, and removing myself from the latent and expressed violence and humiliation in my family and in society at large. How then to unhinge my breastplate and leave my weapons at the door?

About ten years into my recovery, an old friend from New Hampshire finally convinced me to join a workshop the Body Electric School was offering at his retreat center. Celebrating the Body Erotic would be just the thing for me, said Fritz, with all my soul-searching and healing. I was scared that a weekend of getting naked with other men learning Taoist Erotic Massage would pitch me headlong into sex addiction, and I had plenty of other habits, compulsions, and dependencies to contend with.

The workshop was carefully designed to open us gradually by cultivating awareness and becoming more present to ourselves and with each other. Hard work for most of us, but we were ready and we had all the support we needed to guide us through the process. The Body Electric School taught a charging breath that had been developed by Stan and Christina Grof in their psychotherapeutic practice. The breath was also used in rebirthing work I had done earlier in the fall at the suggestion of friends who said it would help my anxiety around buying a house. My experience with the breath work wasn't nearly as powerful as it seemed to be for others.

Apparently I was just getting warmed up.

At the Body Electric workshop, I was in the first group to receive erotic massage, and as the energy built and we intensified the charging breath, my hands and feet cramped, my body temperature dropped, and I felt nauseous. My masseur was frightened, so the assistants stepped in to guide me back to normal breathing and help my body to unclench. Though I was terrified, somehow I knew I was in no real danger. Something in me bore witness to my experience and knew it was an old terror I was remembering. The breath triggered my birth memory, specifically the time when contractions had started but the cervix was still closed, a time when some of the most focused work of birthing begins. My body remembered being in the birth canal without the pushing support of my mother who had been given twilight sleep, an anesthetic that not only relieved pain but which also erased the memory of having given birth at all. On the massage table I'd had the thought: I'm not going to make it. Again, it was a remembered thought more than a current one, as if that were the first thought that had occurred to me, which is to say I didn't think I was going to succeed in getting born at all.

Once back in Maine, I signed up for another rebirthing session with the intention of experiencing full support. I requested three or four helpers to guide me through the breathing practice. They gently supported my head, shoulders, and lower back, and as the intensity built, I heard a very big sound coming out of my body, forcing my throat open, a sharp, high-pitched, sustained cry. From another part of the large room, I heard someone else's voice yelling, "Shut up! Shut up!" And the sound rising from my pelvic floor only got louder. I could feel the hands at my head, shoulders, and back as I began to move, with full support this time, through the birth canal and into the world.

Twelve-step recovery offered me a structure and a process. It was simple and straightforward and provided me with a community of support and the guidance of people who had gone before me—circles of heart and truth-telling. And yet about four years in, I hungered for something I couldn't name. A friend invited me to a Sufi meditation. The practice we were given that first evening was Ya Fazl, an Arabic term meaning, among other things, grace, kindness, favor, and a gift. We repeated it over and over again; it was as if the room were full of bees. Weird, I thought. But then we sat in silence for a time and it was as if the sound I had been making kept sounding silently in my body, a sort of buzz or hum. And that was interesting. There seemed to be no dogma, no special way to fold my legs. No proselytizing, no conversion. I could come as I was; the practices offered were about listening, embodiment, and following the wisdom of the healing heart. A tradition based not on creed but on one's own experience, something I needed to learn how to trust—a lot of work for anyone from an alcoholic family.

I kept attending the meditation classes and then a daylong retreat with Aziza Scott, who offered initiation and became my guide. I trusted both the simplicity and the subtle nuances as I continued to study and practice, which opened me to deeper and deeper encounters with the Divine. I discovered that Sufis were guardians of the mystical heart, not only of Islam but of many other traditions as well—including Christian.

I first encountered Neil Douglas-Klotz's rendition of the Aramaic Lord's Prayer at a dance retreat. As we learned each line and the accompanying steps and movements, my body began to remember—not just the words but their vibration and attunement. Which is what I experienced when I first heard Hebrew chanted and sung at Yom Kippur services and what I experienced in churches when I was in Russia. Every so often, I attended Saturday afternoon mass at a nearby Catholic church. When the priest called us to the table, he didn't include any of the usual disclaimers about those who were disqualified, he simply called everyone to the table, in the way that Jesus had. And so I found myself in line, proceeding to the altar. The priest placed the Host in my hand, I placed it on my tongue and filed back to my seat in the last pew.

Some years later, when I was received into the Catholic Church at Easter Vigil, I could feel five hundred years of ancestral resentment lift and dissolve, and it occurred to me that at long last, the war was over. Which was and was not true.

A few months later, I phoned my priest friend and confessed that every so often during the homily, I wanted to punch the priest in the nose.

"Ah," he said. "Now you're a real Catholic."

When I landed in British Colombia in November 2007, I wanted to find some place I could go on retreat for Christmas. The monastery in Mission was closing for the holidays, but the Bethlehem Centre in Nanaimo was open, so I booked a room.

I arrived midafternoon and had some time in the library before dinner. Since I was the only retreatant and not on silence, the sisters who ran the center invited me to eat with them. In the course of our conversation, I admired their library and said I was surprised to find so many heretical works in it.

Everyone's face went pale and there was silence.

"What I mean is I was glad to see books by Matthew Fox and Mary Daly as well as books by psychologists and sociologists."

They relaxed a bit. You might remember the general atmosphere of the church during Benedict's papacy. The American women religious had not yet been put under doctrinal review, but it was in the air, somehow, and Catholics—even in Canada—were nervous.

The Benedictine Sisters in Nanaimo and the community that had formed around weekly services in the chapel became my first community of faith. My local parish back on the mainland was another story. The priest was painfully shy and could not bring himself to look me in the eye when I shook his hand after mass. No one in the parish talked to me, and when I introduced myself once to someone in the same pew, he said he was new to Vancouver, had been coming to this parish for weeks, and no one had spoken to him either. The homilies where uninspired, the liturgy flat and formulaic. Something I couldn't put my finger on was missing. I figured I wasn't trying hard enough. So after receiving the Host, I would return to my pew, kneel, and watch the others in line, repeating to myself: These are my people, recalling my Hebrew name, Amichai, my people are alive. Until my heart opened, and I could actually feel it.

I had started writing a column for a local online newspaper and decided to write about St. Paul's, an Anglican church in the neighborhood, which had an interesting history. I set up interviews with the priest and various parishioners and decided to attend a service, which was lovely, standard English fare, with hymns I remembered from my time with the Episcopalians in St. Louis when I was in high school.

When it came time to share the peace, people turned to those nearby and shook their hand or nodded, but it didn't stop there. They spilled into the aisle, walked from the back of the church to the front, from the front to the back, hugging, chatting—it went on and on—until the priest had to call us to order so he could get on with the mass.

The thing that was missing in the Roman church down the road was here, and it was Spirit—a delightful sort of anarchy, heart in abundance, friendship. So that became my parish for a few years until, three priests later, it was time to find a new church.

My spiritual director in Vancouver had moved back to his community in the Solomon Islands, and a friend put me onto a Jesuit who served as the second priest in a Catholic parish that offered regular half-day and daylong retreats on Ignatian spiritual practices.

The embodied encounter I'd had with the pre-Christian Yeshua while praying the Aramaic Lord's Prayer never left me, but our relationship remained problematic. He seemed so remote, his story full of gaps. I had a clearer sense of Gilgamesh and Inanna from the Sumerian epics than I had of Jesus from the four Gospels.

During an Ignatian retreat on the Holy Family's flight to Egypt and their return, we were guided to imagine their reunion with Mary's kinswoman Elizabeth, the mother of John the Baptist. I pictured a young adolescent Jesus and his cousin John in conversation. John wants to hear all about his cousin's time in Egypt; he's a bit envious of his adventure. Jesus affects a certain nonchalance, but he can't hide his enthusiasm about the things he saw. Jesus is aware of John's greater physical maturity, and they talk about changes in their bodies. I want to respect their privacy, so I don't listen too closely, but I sense their bewildered excitement, and I hear them laughing. They seem relieved to be talking so openly, and they make a pact: They will always tell the truth about what they experience in their bodies, whether or not that experience becomes part of their public teaching.

John the Baptist is another mysterious character, so I welcomed the opportunity to pray with the story of Jesus's baptism in Matthew for a number of days when I was praying the Ignatian Exercises.

When I picture the scene, I stand with others on the shore, watching. I wonder how long it has been since they have seen each other and sense Jesus's quickened heartbeat, a mixture of fear and excitement. He needs help entering this next phase of his evolution. And somehow it has to be his kinsman who lives in the wilderness and eats locusts and wild honey, his crazy cousin John, whose heart beats even faster. "No," he says. "I can't baptize you; you have to baptize me." It's an awkward moment. Neither man knows how to proceed. Then John seems to say, All right, okay. He takes a deep breath, looks into Jesus's eyes, puts his hands on his shoulder, turns him around, and they wade into deeper water.

I kick off my sandals, hike up my robe, and follow them to get as close as possible. John lowers Jesus into the water and holds him there. I imagine Jesus's ears filling with water, a tightness in his chest, his breath held, heart pounding. Jesus enters the water from a human perspective, this denser element, where a human person cannot survive for long and yet also an element he knows is alive, breathless, murky, full of swift, swimming, floating forms, a beautiful diffused light, sounds and colors unknown to the upper world, alien and yet necessary to all physical and psychic life, one of the places where we encounter soul.

John raises his cousin out of the water. Jesus opens his eyes, his lungs release the old air, and he takes a deep fresh breath as the heavens open and God says, "This is my son, with whom I am well pleased."

Mikvah, ritual bathing, purification.

In the first dream I remember having as a child, I slide down a chute into water. A bare-chested man stands waist-deep, and pushes my head below the surface. He's laughing. I wake up screaming and gasping for air.

For years I puzzled over the dream, different interpretations opening to me at different stages of my life and understanding. It suggested the difficulty I experienced at birth, my struggle for survival. It suggested something about my father and how oppressed I felt by him. The male figure seemed malevolent. And yet, the dream also suggests a kind of baptism, an initiation. But into what?

At some point, I worked with the dream by voicing tones I associated with the movement in the dream—the slide down the chute, then the deeper movement into the water. A short tune emerged. I raised and then lowered my left hand, the movement down the chute, and then my right hand pressed farther down, the movement into the water. As I repeated these gestures, I noticed that at the end of the descent of my right hand, my left hand rose to begin the movement anew. My attention was drawn to the space between the two motions—the end of one, the beginning of the next. The submerging action was not the end of the story. The movement was not only down into the water but also back up again. I began to experience the dream differently. Death, yes, maybe, but also rebirth. Entering and emerging from a watery depth, the unconscious realm, dream and shadow, which by the time I was in my mid-fifties, I had come to accept as a central task in my life: to make the descent and to resurface with new insight.

During my immersion in the mikvah, I felt myself cleansed not only of personal impurities but also the anti-Semitism of my gentile ancestors—the pogroms, the forced conversions, and the Holocaust during the Second World War. I was still accountable. I had a role to play in reconciliation. I was being initiated into the practice of tikkun olam, repairing the world.

And when I was baptized as a Catholic, I was releasing layers and layers of bitter resentment, which had plagued my protestant family for generations.

These rituals of purification, cleansing, and release were an essential part of a process I'd begun as a schoolboy—healing the splits and schisms within and between the three branches of the Abrahamic line. The ongoing religious wars were emblematic of a profound soul sickness seeking a cure. I can do nothing about the conflicts in the world outside without addressing the war within. No amount of cognitive gymnastics was going to pull together the splinters of my own soul, let alone the world soul. I had to embody this peace initiative. I had to live it with every fiber of my being.

The 2015 Spiritual Directors International Annual Conference in Louisville, Kentucky, was the most broadly interfaith gathering I had ever attended. My friend Mary, an American nun, had called me to the practice of spiritual direction while we were designing a leadership seminar for Australian women religious. She'd seen something in me and named it, and my heart sank. I didn't know what a spiritual director was. It sounded way too churchy, and I wasn't up for getting trained and certified in yet another thing. But this thing was different, and I knew it. I realized I had experienced what Christians call spiritual direction with my guide in the Sufi Order—and with various sponsors in twelve-step programs. I learned that the practice of spiritual direction was one of the missing pieces of the Christian tradition I'd been looking for.

And in a number of ways my formation had already begun. I sought further training in Vancouver, starting with the Catholic Archdiocese, who seemed baffled by my question. Formation and training in spiritual direction? We have nothing like that. "But you guys invented it!" I said. No luck. I was to learn that laypeople called to the ministry of spiritual direction are in a precarious position in relation to the church—Catholic, Anglican, and Protestant—because we are self-governing and guided by the Holy Spirit. If that weren't enough to worry the clerics, we are a broad-based interfaith movement and, for all the talk about their brothers and sisters in other faith traditions, even simple ecumenism makes most churches nervous.

Off to Australia we went, Sister Mary and I, and in the course of the seminar, she told the story of how American women religious found out they were being put under doctrinal review—someone announced it at a press conference before the Leadership Conference of Women Religious was notified. She described a flurry of text messaging all across the United States and emergency meetings of communities to discuss and discern their response. This was my first time hearing the story, and I struggled not to show emotion as I listened, onstage next to the podium. The Australian sisters showed no such compunction and spoke their minds quite freely once the microphone was making its rounds. The story was a discreet warning to Australian women religious leaders to be prepared should the Vatican's doctrinal review be extended to their communities.

By April 2015, the Leadership Conference of Women Religious had been under doctrinal review for six years. On the second morning of the Spiritual Directors International conference, someone came to the podium and said there was an important announcement to be made before introducing the first speaker of the day. A Sister of Mercy stepped forward. "The doctrinal review of the Leadership Conference of Women Religious has been canceled. The controversy is over." We rose to our feet and applauded, tears streaming down the faces of people who didn't even know what a doctrinal review was—Buddhist monks, Protestant pastors, Hindus, Sufis, Muslims, rabbis. The upswell of love and affirmation for the American Sisters was something I will never forget—and it confirmed that I was where I belonged, among people committed to creating new communities of contemplative response in a new spirit of unity and kinship.

Meanwhile, I was in uncharted territory, which was becoming increasingly hostile and fraught with danger as the world continued to splinter and descend into political and social chaos. And yet the collapse of an empire nearly always coincides with a rise in new thought, the reclamation of ancient wisdom, and new forms of expression. Theologies of certainty and their old maps don't serve us, so once again we rely on other forms of guidance and tools of navigation. Signs and portents, stars, wind, the flight of birds, Spirit, the ancestors. As the astrologer and visionary activist Caroline Casey often reminds us: Allies are everywhere.

I first heard about Mirabai Starr through friends in Taos, New Mexico. She was something of a legend. It wasn't until I read her book *Caravan of No Despair: A Memoir of Loss and Transformation,* that I began to feel a deeper kinship with her. We both had powerful spiritual initiations after the death of a loved one. We both have searched and struggled, and found ways of integrating disparate, often conflicting theologies.

At the onset of the Covid lockdown, I joined an online course she offered on women mystics. She gave me a precious gift in those weeks. Her teaching brought together threads from the world's great wisdom traditions and wove them into a discernable pattern. It went beyond her rigorous scholarship; her whole life had been a deep dive into devotional practices. Her experience and teaching validated my own crazy spiritual path with its tangents and divergences. Like many seekers, she had been warned against drawing from more than one spiritual tradition.

Teachers from every tradition directed her to chose one path and follow it to its deep heart, not flit from one to another, which, of course, is good advice as far as it goes. But many of us knew something was missing in the traditions we were raised in or the ones we had chosen to follow after leaving home. And to be sure we've often been foolish and thoughtless and failed to properly respect and understand the traditions we were exploring. We were young, after all. But our hunger and longing were deep, our love was ardent, and we persisted, not only in interfaith dialogue but in sharing the actual practices—devotional, contemplative, esoteric, and healing—not to steal them but to keep them alive. I join others in believing that the danger of withholding these practices far outweighs the risk of their commodification.

I think of a story sometimes told in Sufi circles about Christian Crusaders and Muslim soldiers meeting in secret to exchange esoteric teachings and mystical practices—and how Islamic mysticism found its way into Europe, infused the poetry of the troubadours and the tradition of courtly love. Islamic poets were reawakening a Christian mystical heart that was in danger of disappearing altogether.

Later I was given an opportunity to pray the Ignatian Spiritual Exercises, guided by Lois Zachariah, a spiritual director in Ontario. Drawing from the work of the Jesuits John English and Teilhard de Chardin, the biologist and Franciscan Sister Ilia Delio, Indigenous wisdom, and biosemiotics, Lois and her husband Kuruvila came up with an expression of the Spiritual Exercises they called the Green Christ, which reflected the emergence of a more holistic ecological cosmology, yet remained faithful to the language and spirit of Saint Ignatius's original intentions.

Over the next nine months, I struggled with Ignatius's militarism and sixteenth-century Spanish colonial worldview, and through those struggles, something opened, shifted and deepened in me. With the help of my twelve-step experience, Sufi and Buddhist practices, and Jewish wisdom, I could sink beneath my discursive mind and enter my heart. Through repetition, praying with the imagination, and the practice of colloquy, or prayerful dialogue, I brought my objections, opinions, resentments, and wounds directly to Yeshua, and his responses were always surprising.

When directed to pray with Matthew 26:36–46, I find myself in the garden of Gethsemane. When Jesus scolds us a third time for falling asleep and then says, "Get up. Let's go," I say, "Wait a minute," and taking Jesus aside, I say, "Look. We're exhausted. Give us a break. We're afraid." When I look at Jesus, I see tears streaming down his face. We sit in silence and weep. I wonder where Magdalena is when we need her.

"We have no idea how to go on without you," I say.

"The women will teach you how to grieve," says Jesus.

While praying the Spiritual Exercises, I accompanied a friend through the last stages of his cancer. He lived upcountry and we spoke on the phone. He was often in pain, often despondent, and ambivalent about medically assisted death. I listened; my heart ached. I felt relieved, even exalted when he had good days. He'd been an outdoorsman all his life, hiking, skiing, active in community wildlife conservation groups. As his illness progressed, he had more and more trouble walking. Once he got a mobility scooter, he could manage the level parts of the trails he loved. He dreamed of designing hikes and excursions into the wilderness for those who couldn't walk. Sometimes I asked him to take me on one of those trails in his imagination, describing what I might see and hear, the different fragrances in the air. Other times he entered a different terrain, part memory, part dream, a stone ledge above a clear lake where he would wait for an elder, a spirit healer he knew would meet him and guide him.

He'd worked mostly as a carpenter and cabinetmaker and told me that in his next life he wanted to come back as a wood carver—like Robert Davidson, whose work I didn't know. He pointed me to a documentary about Davidson and his work called *Haida Modern.* I didn't get a chance to see it until Holy Week that year—two weeks after my friend died.

In the last section of the Spiritual Exercises, one contemplates Christ's Passion, Crucifixion, and Resurrection. Early in Haida Modern, there's footage of people coming together in 1969 and raising the first totem pole in Haida Gwaii in almost a hundred years. Davidson carved that pole with the help of his brother, Reg, and he describes the strange absence of carved objects, never mind the poles when he started work in Haida Gwaii. Almost everything had disappeared, and some resisted the idea of raising a new pole, fearing reprisals from both church and crown.

I watched the film a number of times, trying to get my head around all that had happened. I'd been living in British Columbia for nearly fifteen years, and I knew nothing about any of this. What moved me most was the image of the raising itself. Men from different bands shouldering the pole while others pushed with beams of timber, and still others pulled from the other side with ropes. Slowly, gradually, like a heart learning to pulse blood again, it rose, and I was struck by the contrast between this image of new life and the pole Jesus carried by himself to his own execution.

"The tone of the pole raising was amazing," says Davidson in the film. "I didn't realize the celebration was really uncorking the bottle—how the old people carried themselves, how they talked, how they danced, how they sang songs. It spoke volumes of the knowledge that was still with them, the knowledge that survived. It was like the culture was never ever gone. It was open. I had no idea how important it was, how this would be affecting many people outside of the Haida Nation . . . The totem pole was actually a catalyst to make a statement that hey we're alive, and we want to be part of this world."

The image became for me a new image of resurrection—of an entire community and culture, a reawakened people, in the process of restoring balance.

In June 2021, there were 182 unmarked graves discovered near a former residential school outside Cranbrook, British Columbia. While no one was entirely surprised, I was horrified— as an American, I already carried the shame of slavery and genocidal wars against Native Americans.

And now this. The thing the crown and the church hoped had been dealt with and buried was pushing its way through the earth to let us know it was not finished. It took time for me to distinguish my shame and outrage from the grief I felt for those children and their families and my own sense of being betrayed by the church. It was like living with an alcoholic who swears up and down he's not drinking, and yet you keep finding bottles behind the furnace.

I joined the large online gatherings led by Indigenous elders. It was good to see more clearly the history I now carried as a Canadian citizen. The work of reconciliation, which had been overshadowed by other issues, was once more front and center. The elders reminded us of the importance of strong support and creating safe places for feeling and expressing pain in ways that did no harm. As important as legislative changes and other forms of reparation were, we needed—Indigenous people and settlers alike—a deep substantive healing of our bodies, hearts, and souls, and to release our ancestors from any pain they were still holding.

St. James' is an Anglian parish in downtown Vancouver. A mix of Art Deco, Romanesque, Byzantine, and Gothic Revival, the present and third building was consecrated in 1938. For a few years, I saw a spiritual director who lived in the building next door. Sister Mary and I had recently returned from the leadership seminar in Australia, and Brother John had returned to Canada from the Solomon Islands.

I tried to describe what it was like to walk on land that was older than God. What it was like to see birds and plants I'd never seen before or even knew existed. What it was like to feel Spirit pulsing up from the earth into my legs—and how the Catholic Sisters were not at odds with Aboriginal spirit, and how they had to walk this perilous path between church and crown like running some kind of gauntlet. And yet they stood firm in the truth and mystery of their dreaming. I wanted Brother John to explain all this to me, but he didn't have much to say. Not that he avoided the subject. He seemed to know exactly what I was trying to describe, but it was, in some final sense, beyond words—certainly English words. It was something he had come to embody over the years, a medicine he carried and dispensed to us without our knowing, but after sitting with him I was altered somehow, more at ease, certainly, but there was something else. It was as if he were opening my capacity to hold something not of this world, something which belonged to an earth wisdom far older than anything I could imagine, and which also felt like memory.

After sitting with Brother John, I would attend the noontime mass next door at St. James'. Each time I stepped into the church, it's as if I were stepping out of this world and into a stark and sacred place in an indistinct but ancient time, with winter light filtering through a smudged window high in a stone wall.

St. James' is one of those Christian paradoxes—High Church liturgy in the midst of the city's most visible suffering; a complex relationship with Indigenous peoples in the area and a shared deep commitment to the difficult work of listening and surrendering again and again to love.

It's midnight mass on Christmas Eve. I find a pew and kneel. All at once I'm in a stone church in sixteenth-century England, a French Protestant, seeking mercy, safety, knowing that this church bearing the name of the patron saint of pilgrims is just another stop along the way. I am grateful on behalf of my ancestors who sought and found refuge, and continued to wander, called to a new life, driven by fear, ambition, hope, dreams, visions, and crazy wisdom. I feel them with me, singing, these citizens of heaven, as we stand in wonder and confront once again the awe-filled mystery of the birth of the Beloved.

After mass, I greet friends, wish them merry Christmas, shake hands with the priests, and make my way through the homeless encampment to the bus stop in Chinatown. But it's late, there won't be many buses, so I turn and rejoin the caravan of souls following Khidr, the Green One who guided Moses, guided in turn by Sophia, Shekinah, and the archangel who some say wrestled Jacob to the ground. Accompanied by the whistle of a distant freight train, the sound of ankle bells, and muffled drums, we keep on walking.

Next of Kin

When I get to the intensive care unit at the hospital in Des Peres, Missouri, I find Patty wired to several machines that beep softly. Her eyes are open. She recognizes me but has difficulty speaking. The beginnings of sentences come out all right, but the ends are chewed and garbled. Her jaw moves up and down involuntarily. I have to listen hard and ask her to repeat. Her breathing is labored. I don't want to make her talk more than she has to.

She doesn't know what happened to her. All her friend in the retirement community said when I called was something about her kidneys. Something about being incoherent.

"Well," Patty says, "here—we—are. Nothing—to—do—but—wait—I—guess."

I imagine she'd shrug if she could.

"This is a fine how do you do," she might say if speaking were easier.

The nurse, Dave, explains that Patty was on a ventilator, but is now breathing on her own. Improved compared to when they brought her in. My sense is that she's dying.

He asks if I am her closest living relative, and I have to think a moment. Patty Mansfield is my mother's cousin. I run it through my mind: an only child, no children of her own, no nieces or nephews. I suppose I am. Patty had been my grandfather's favorite niece. For some reason, my mother never liked her.

I met Patty when she attended a reading I gave in St. Louis some years ago. She came up to me afterward and introduced herself. Nearly every time I've gone to St. Louis since then, we've managed to have lunch or meet at Schneithorst's for breakfast. I would always invite my mother to come along, but she'd grow evasive and decline.

Patty and I have had similar lives. We're both writers, both worked for a time in advertising, and neither of us married. Even today unmarried people are viewed with condescending sympathy and a certain amount of suspicion. Envy, I think. Of our independence. As if we had cheated. Shirked some essential duty of adulthood.

When she finished college at the start of World War II, Patty joined the navy. She told her mother first.

"If it had been me at your age, I'd have enlisted too," her mother said, without even looking up from her knitting.

Then she told her father, who threw a fit. "No daughter of mine . . . !" That sort of thing.

Patty earned the rank of lieutenant and trained officers in Washington, DC. She carried top-secret orders—on the train up and down the East Coast, and by plane to California.

On the second day that I visit her in the hospital, she is neither asleep nor entirely awake. Her eyes are slightly open, but she's not seeing me. I've brought a photograph of her favorite uncle, my grandfather, after whom I am named. I'd found it among the things my brother and sister and I had been going through the day before.

I stand by Patty's bed, praying. I hum the old hymn "Softly and Tenderly Jesus Is Calling." It's all I can think to do. I don't want to wake her. She seems to be resting comfortably. Though her breathing is even more labored than the day before, she is not struggling. She seems unafraid. Over the course of our friendship, I've learned that she's a woman who goes to her Protestant church every Sunday, the most ordinary kind of religious observance. Conventional. There has never been a hint of rancor or resentment over my mother's snubs or the complicated social strata of St. Louis. She never made a fuss over her independence. She showed normal pride in her accomplishments as an advertising account executive and one of the founders of the St. Louis Women's Advertising Club, which raised nearly twice the amount for charity one year as the Men's Advertising Club.

She has lived by her own lights, followed her own mind and heart, always curious about the world. She doesn't regret anything. At least not anything she's willing to tell me.

The doctor comes in to check on her and again I'm asked if I am her closest living relative. I reckon I am. There is no living will, nor is there anyone they know of who has power of attorney. That's why they keep asking me. In cases like these, they put together an Ethics Committee to decide if treatment ought to be continued.

All I can say is what I see: my friend and second cousin, unafraid, following her failing heart toward home.

Acknowledgments

In January of 2019, I rented an L-shaped room with good light, a galley kitchen, and a washroom. I brought in a table, a folding chair, a desk lamp, a kettle, a coffee mug, and a radio. I sat down, rolled a fresh sheet of paper into my manual typewriter, and started typing.

What's important here is that I had no objective, no agenda, no project in mind other than to create designated space for – well – listening, really. No phone. No WiFi. No email. No Google. No Siri. Nothing beeped or blinked or tried in any way to call my attention away from the task at hand: following thought, memory, sound, image, inkling, notion, grievance, gripe and awe – as one led to another and circled back again. When I reached the bottom of a page, I pulled it out, numbered it, put it in a box, and rolled in another sheet of paper.

Toward the end of the year, I read through the pages in the box, pen in hand, looking for themes, repetitions. Here and there I found thoughts about drawing, so I marked them, took a fresh piece of paper, rolled it into the machine and headed into a first draft of what became "Drawing and Talent". Four drafts later I was ready to bring it home, type it into the computer and send it off to artists I knew who might be interested. As each essay came into something like a final form, I'd send it off to people who might like to read it, and they sent back their own thoughts on the subject. Essays tend to open conversations on a topic – a call and response. And so the essays began to make their way into the world.

I want to thank those first readers for their insights and enthusiasm – their willingness to share their own perspectives, memories, and experiences.

Thanks to my trusty Olympia manual typewriter, a high school graduation gift from my Uncle Tom in 1970.

To the fellow in West Vancouver who still cleans and repairs typewriters, and to a company somewhere in China that still makes typewriter ribbons, my heartfelt thanks.

Were it not for CBC radio hosts Tom Allen and Paolo Pietro Paolo, each of whom set up a home studio in order to keep on broadcasting through lockdowns, I don't know what kind of shape I'd been in today. They were my companions and kept me connected to fellow cultural workers in the world outside the eight or nine city blocks I inhabited during those long months.

It wasn't until I had written about a dozen essays that I began to think I might have a book – and it wasn't until I put them together and sent them to my editor, and she sent them back with her first edits that I read the essays as a book, and it wasn't until my third reading – slowly, out loud, reviewing each edit and then noticing things I wanted to change myself – that I had any real sense of what I'd written. I had to be in conversation with it myself – listening, questioning, and responding.

Thank you, Karla Eoff, for once again inviting me into that conversation and helping me to coax the book into its final form.

My thanks to those who agreed to read and respond to the book as a whole: my colleague and old friend novelist Agnes Bushell, former Maine Poet Laureate and director of the Haystack Mountain School of Crafts Stuart Kestenbaum, metalsmith, author, and publisher Tim McCreight, champion of right relationship, and co-founder of CRR Global, Faith Fuller, community-based theatre artist Will Weigler, poet and community activator Kevin Spenst, artist, actor, and bouffon provocateur, Trilby Jeeves. And to any number of others who have supported this project indirectly through their love and support – colleague, mentor, friend and neighbor (despite the 3,000 miles that separate our houses) Allice Haidden; Canadian colleagues, friends, and co-conspirators Shelley Reid, Janet Frood, David Frank Gomes, Lois and Kuruvila Zachariah, Leslie Ross, Keith Brydges, Rodger Reynolds, Chris Dorey, Sequoia Thom, David Hoe, John Neffenger, Achille Gardillini, David Konst, Lucia Gamroth, the Gillese family, and my guide and steady companion in prayer Father Bill Wilson, S.J.

And – of course – to UNH professor Don Murry, without whose deep listening, curiosity, and keen insights, my writing life might never have been.

Colophon

Design and layout by Tim McCreight, Brynmorgen Press using the fonts Adobe Garamond Pro and LTC Bodoni 175 Pro.

The printed edition was manufactured in the United States; the digital edition was created by Booqlab of Barcelona, Spain.

www.ingramcontent.com/pod-product-compliance
Lightning Source LLC
Chambersburg PA
CBHW031304120726
47906CB00003B/877

* 9 7 8 1 0 6 8 9 8 2 6 0 6 *